Sis Tiffany Black

MW00880646

Riches of Grace

A Compilation of Experiences in the Christian Life—A
Narration of Trials and Victories Along the Way

BY E. E. BYRUM

By grace are ye saved through faith.—Eph 2:8.

Let us therefore come boldly unto the throne of grace, that
we may obtain mercy, and find grace to help in time of
need.—Heb. 4:16.

Originally published in 1918.

CONTENTS

Author's Preface

To be right with God and to have a constant knowledge of his approval is the desire of every Christian. Many people deep in sin and others honest at heart have a longing to live a righteous life, but they have always found obstacles in their pathway and have been defeated in every attempt.

In the preparation of this volume the author has aimed to refer to such obstacles and hindrances in the lives of others, so that any one passing through a trial or laboring under a heavy burden or oppression may, by reading these narratives, learn how to find relief.

A lady who was victor over many trials and impositions of the enemy, and who knew that I had been passing through some severe ordeals, said to me: "It does me good, and is a source of great encouragement, even to know that you and others who are supposed to be strong in faith have trials and severe testings occasionally." It is hoped that the trials and the victories mentioned herein will be not only a source of encouragement to others but such an inspiration to their faith that they will be enabled to understand and do the will of God.

This book is a compilation of experiences from people in various parts of the world who have written by special request of the author. The fact that they were written by people in China, India, Australia, Egypt, West Indies, and other countries, is evidence that although the environment and circumstances may differ, yet God is everywhere the same to fulfil the promises given in his Word, in all countries and among the people of every nation. Although the names and addresses are not given, the experiences are genuine, and the author will take pleasure in furnishing information concerning any of them.

The "Experience of a Hundred Years Ago," given on page 245 was taken from an old book that in my early childhood days I often saw my mother read. The book was old and worn long before I was born, and I have only a few pages as a relic of early remembrances. It was entitled "The Riches of Grace."

No doubt the title of this old book, together with a knowledge of the comfort and consolation that my mother received from reading the many Christian experiences it contained, contributed to my inspiration in presenting these pages for the benefit of others.

I hereby acknowledge my indebtedness and heartfelt thanks to those who have so kindly contributed to this compilation of experiences, and I trust that every burdened soul that reads these experiences may take courage and may henceforth abound in the riches of the grace of God.

Yours for a victorious life,

E. E. BYRUM.

Anderson, Indiana, January 16, 1918.

The Joy and Blessings of a Christian Life

EXPERIENCE NUMBER 1

The pathway of life has its shadows and sunshine, its pleasures and sorrows; and in the Christian life, I am convinced, many people live in the shadow more than in the sunshine, when they could very well have it otherwise.

When I was about thirteen years of age, I yielded myself to the Lord and made a decision to spend my life in his service. Since that time, like Christian in Bunyan's "Pilgrim's Progress," I have met with many and varied experiences; but one beautiful encouraging thought has been that, no matter how hard my trials, how near my strength was gone, nor how little my courage lacked of failing, just at that time, when I was the most helpless, God was always present to help either by his Spirit or by sending one of his servants to encourage and strengthen me.

I have, indeed, found the Christian life to be a warfare. Every individual who enlists in the service of the Lord will have the forces of evil to battle against, but God has made provision whereby every child of God can be an overcomer in every conflict. The one who has a firm decision to be true at any cost will receive such power and help that Satan can not prevent him from serving the Lord. The enemy may try to hinder by causing trials, difficulties, and perplexities, and at times the way may seem dark, with no apparent hope of day; but our God, who is mighty, will turn all these seeming hindrances into real blessings and make them stepping-stones to glory.

In my youthful days I felt a deep desire to work for God and longed to fill some place in life where I could feel that I not only was living a life of salvation, but was really engaged in my Master's service. As I knelt in earnest prayer and consecrated myself fully to the Lord for him to direct me as seemed best, a dark sorrow filled my heart; for Satan whispered: "You are too young. You can not stand against the powers of evil that all young people must meet. Your covenant with the Lord is too great for you to keep." But with tears I cried unto the Lord to know if these suggestions were true. At that moment the Lord gave me the assurance that if I decided to serve him he would teach me how to do so. He would give me grace in every time of need.

Some time after this I became very ill and knew unless God came to my aid I should soon have to leave this world. As I thought of my condition, a joy filled my soul that I might soon be with the Lord. With this joy came also a sadness, as I realized that I had done nothing in the vineyard of the Lord. It seemed that I could not bear to go empty-handed. I prayed God to spare my life that I might work for him. He graciously and instantly touched my body with his healing power, and in a few days I was able to attend school.

Once I was about to make a decision and take a step that would have hindered me from filling the place the Lord designed I should fill. At that moment the Lord made known to me by his Holy Spirit in such a way that I could not question his leadings that he had called me to his service, and also made known to me the place that I was chosen to fill. Immediately I was reminded of my covenant with the Lord, although I had to stand against the pleadings and earnest entreaties of some of my very dear friends.

Before this I had decided not to leave my mother, but to work near my home so that I could readily respond in case of sickness. After considerable meditation about the matter of leaving my father and mother, brothers and sisters, in order to take up my work for the Lord, the matter became very serious. Finally I went to the Lord one morning in earnest prayer. I shall never forget that season of prayer, when I seemed to be in the direct presence of the Lord. My consecration was put to a test as one question after another was presented, as to whether or not I should be willing to die, to really give my life, if God so designed, that my unsaved loved ones might be saved, or to do the same for lost souls who were not dear to me according to the ties of nature. And again, should I be willing to give my life for lost sinners and have them scoff and spurn me? These were hard questions, but my heart said: "Lord, thy will be done. Where thou leadest I will follow." I was solemnly impressed with the thought: Jesus came to save a lost world, but they crucified him; instead of accepting his love, they rejected it.

Within a short time I had the matter settled beyond a doubt that the time had come for me to enter upon the mission whereunto the Lord had called me. The way began to open before me, and as I bid loved ones farewell, a sweet assurance filled my soul that my decision and action was in accordance with His will. It gave me much sorrow to leave home, but God so blessed and directed me that I have never been sorry that I obeyed his voice. Over and over I have proved that God's way is best. His way may cause pain and sorrow at times, which we may not be able to understand, but in the end we can know of a truth that God has caused all things to work together for our good and for his glory.

At one time I was very much tested, and discouragements presented themselves. I was trying hard to be an overcomer and to cast every burden upon the Lord. The enemy would suggest that it was of no use for me to try to stand against the things that were oppressing me and that it would be better to surrender, and even give place to discouragements, and that even though I should come out a conqueror later, no one would ever know anything about it. At first this suggestion seemed plausible, but upon further consideration I said: "No, I will not surrender. If no one else ever knows, I will know, God will know, and the devil will know, that I stood true and came out victorious." This experience has since that time often been a real encouragement to me.

At another time I had for weeks been passing through real testing times. Occasionally the trials would lift and God would bless my soul, but again the darkness of depressions would settle over me. I began to weary and to long for deliverance. The suggestion came that it would be better for me to cease serving God and never to try again. Over and over something whispered that there was no use to continue; that if others who were older and better qualified fell by the wayside and could not stand, there was positively no use in my trying. Finally the enemy insisted that there was nothing else for me to do than to give up, and that, after all, I was in a deplorable spiritual condition; that there was no hope for me. At this point I discerned that it was the enemy, and, kneeling before God, I promised him that if he could get more glory out of my life by my being in such a trial all the rest of my days, I was willing to submit to the trial. When I came to this decision my trial vanished suddenly, and God poured the glory into my soul and the victory was far sweeter than the trial had been bitter.

Sometimes I have had trials in which I could see no good nor from which I could not perceive how any good could possibly result; but later I would be enabled to know that those very trials were worth more to me than any treasure this earth could afford.

As I look upon my past life and see how mercifully God has dealt with me, how he has guided and protected, and how he has shielded me from the power of the tempter, my heart cries out, "What a mighty God! What a great and loving Father!" Counting my blessings, I find they so far outnumber my trials that it brings me real courage to press on, knowing, as I do, that grace will be given me to meet whatever may yet lie in my pathway. "For there hath no temptation taken you but such as is common to man: but God is faithful, who will not suffer you to be tempted above that ye are able; but will with the temptation also make a way to escape, that ye may be able to bear it" (1 Cor. 10:13).

Experiences of a Minister

EXPERIENCE NUMBER 2

A careworn woman once asked a philosopher how she might obtain relief from and victory over the trials and sorrows of life. He said to her, "Fetch me a cup of salt from some home where sorrow and care has never entered, and I will then tell you the secret of victory." After a long and weary journey, she returned to him saying that she had given up the search in despair; for in all her travels she found no home entirely free from care and sorrow. Like this poor woman, I once longed and sought for some state or condition in life where I might be free from the cares and perplexities that distressed me, but my search too seemed fruitless. At last, after many disappointments, I found the more excellent way of victory over my trials through simple, trusting faith in Him who notes even the sparrow's fall.

Before I fully learned this lesson, there were times in my life when it seemed I was on the verge of despair, so severe were my trials. As I now look back to those scenes and experiences, there come to my mind the pathetic lines of Longfellow's poem "The Bridge."

For my heart was hot and restless,

And my life was full of care,

And the burden laid upon me

Seemed greater than I could bear.

But now it has fallen from me,

It is buried in the sea;

And only the sorrow of others

Throws its shadow over me.

And I think how many thousands

Of care-encumbered men,

Each bearing his burden of sorrow,

Have crossed the bridge since then.

For the sake of the many thousands who are still trying to bear their own burdens, I send forth the following account of some of my life's experiences. I trust the Lord may use it to help some on their way to the feet of Him who said, "Come unto me, all ye that labor and are heavy-laden, and I will give you rest" (Matt. 11:28).

There are doubtless thousands whose sins have been forgiven, but who have not yet learned by actual experience the precious privilege expressed in these words: "Casting all your care upon him, for he careth for you" (1 Pet. 5:7). An old lady was once trudging along a hot and dusty highway carrying a heavy basket. She was soon overtaken by a kind man, who invited her to take a seat in the rear of his carriage. After some time had passed, he looked back to see how his passenger was getting along, when he was astonished to see her holding that heavy basket on her lap. "Grandma," said he, "there is plenty of room; why do you not set your basket down?" "Oh," she replied, "you are so kind to take me in that I thought I would make the load as light as possible for your horses, so I concluded to carry the basket myself." We may smile at her reply, yet many who have trusted the Lord to forgive their sins, are nevertheless trying still to carry their own burdens.

MY CONVERSION

In early childhood I was taught to pray and to reverence God's Word. I was deeply impressed with the truths that I learned at Sunday-school. Even as a child I loved the preaching-service, and the Word of God made a strong and lasting impression upon my mind.

When I was about ten years old, a revival was held in my home community. At an afternoon service, held especially for the children, I responded to the altar-call, and there I was completely broken up, the tears running in profusion down my face. My dear mother knelt by my side: "My boy," she said, "if you should desire anything good that I could bestow upon you, would you ask me for it?" I promptly replied in the affirmative. "Then," she continued, "would you believe that your request would be granted?" Again I answered in the affirmative. "That is the way to receive God's blessings," she said. "Now, when you ask the Lord to forgive your sins, believe that he hears and answers your prayer." In simple, child-like faith I believed the promise, and the peace of God gently flooded my soul. One of the most prominent features of my childhood experience was the peculiar love I felt for every one. I longed to see my companions saved.

EARLY TRIALS

Soon after my conversion and before that special series of meetings closed, I heard the pastor relate the experience of a certain boy who had sought and found the Lord. He said that after a period of earnest seeking, all the darkness was instantly dispelled and the boy was wonderfully saved. Judging from this vivid description, I decided that the boy must have witnessed some sudden manifestation of light. Immediately I began to doubt my experience. I was still more disturbed when I saw older persons struggling night after night at the altar and then finally experiencing some powerful emotions which seemed to be far more wonderful than anything that I had experienced. Sometimes I wished that I too might go to the altar again and pray and struggle until some wonderful demonstration should be given to me; but I was naturally backward and timid, and could scarcely make up my mind to go through such an ordeal of struggling as I had witnessed in some of more mature years.

ENCOURAGEMENTS

Although at times I was greatly distressed, yet often when I was in secret prayer, my heart was greatly comforted and I experienced seasons of quiet, peaceful blessings. I noticed, too, that some who had wonderful outward demonstrations at the time they were converted, did not hold out very long, but soon drifted back into sin, while in my own heart the desire still remained to be true to the Lord.

CONFLICTS

I did not, however, enjoy constant victory. At times I gave way to ill-temper or selfish motives. My conscience being tender, I often felt instant condemnation after yielding to these things, and then I would pour out my heart in secret prayer for forgiveness and for grace and strength to resist the temptation more successfully the next time. I remember, also, occasions when, upon the approach of temptation, I would steal away to the secret place of prayer and ask for strength to keep me sweet in my soul. I could then go forth to meet my trials with the utmost calmness and serenity, and victory then seemed easy.

Although I had a Christian home, yet sorrows and trials came into my young life, very painful ones at times. How often I would seek the place of prayer and there in simple, child-like faith unburden my heart to the Lord. Whenever I called upon him, he always gave me relief and never failed to provide a way of escape from every temptation and difficulty.

"In seasons of distress and grief,

My soul has often found relief,

And oft escaped the tempter's snare,
By thy return, sweet hour of prayer."

HEALING

Although I had never received any definite teaching on the subject of divine healing, yet almost intuitively, it seems, I would call upon the Lord for help when afflicted, and would receive the needed help. Several times my mother seemed to be at the point of death. With troubled heart, I sought the place of prayer to tell the Lord all about it. My heart was comforted, my prayers were answered, and Mother was spared.

CALL TO THE MINISTRY

Even in childhood I learned to pray and to testify in public. At first these things were very hard for me, owing to my timid disposition. However, I was always blessed in the effort. The impression came to me early in life that some day I should preach the gospel; in fact, I would occasionally find myself mentally addressing an imaginary audience. Many of my acquaintances also were impressed that the ministry would be my life-work.

DRIFTING

As time went on, formality again found its way into our meetings, and I also imbibed its spirit. My conscience was no longer as tender as it had been, and I actually indulged in things that were sinful. Still I kept up my profession, attended the services, testified and prayed in public, and was generally counted a good Christian.

CONVICTION

At last a humble man of God became our pastor. Without fear, and yet in gentleness and meekness, he preached the Word of God as far as he had light. As I sat under his preaching, the truth went straight to my heart, and I began to see my lack. The revival meeting had now begun, and I saw that I must either serve God in earnest, obeying him in all things, or quit professing.

RECLAIMED

One night after services, while on the way to my room, I resolved to get where the Lord would have me to be even if I should have to pray all night. I began; but the more I prayed the worse I felt. I was shown one thing after another that I should have to give up or make right if I would enjoy God's favor. About the midnight hour, I had said the last yes to God, and then came the test of faith. That very evening I had heard the minister instructing seekers to give up all sin, to ask God's forgiveness, and then to believe his promise that he forgives and saves, whether any change was noticed in the feelings or not; and although I had always longed for the great emotions I thought others had experienced, yet in the absence of any particular feeling, I was willing to believe God's promise.

When I first began to pray, I was conscious of a great deal of fear, which deepened until it seemed I was almost in despair; but as I yielded my will to God's will, all fears subsided, and just before I grasped the promise, I was void of any particular emotion. It seemed to please the Lord to take this plan to teach me that, after all, salvation does not come by feeling. Then calmly and quietly I laid hold upon the promise, "If we confess our sins, he is faithful and just to forgive us our sins, and to cleanse us from all unrighteousness" (1 John 1:9). I said to the Lord, "Now I am willing to forsake all sin and do all thou wouldst have me to do; and although I do not feel any great change, yet I believe that, according to thy Word, thou dost save me now." Quietly but earnestly I said from the depths of my heart, "Jesus saves me now." In a short time the peace of God gently flooded my soul, and I knew that my sins were forgiven.

After spending some time in peaceful communion with God, I went to sleep, knowing beyond a doubt that if I should never awaken, my spirit would immediately take its flight to the realms of the blest. In my gratitude, the tears streamed down my face, and I wondered how I had ever been content to live at such a distance from God as I had lived during the past few years.

CONFLICT WITH DOUBTS

When I awoke the next morning, the peace of God was still in my soul; but Satan faintly whispered, "Perhaps, after all, you were mistaken last night; you may not have a genuine experience of salvation." He suggested also, "You do not feel quite so joyful as you did." In spite of all this, I knew that a great change had taken place in me. Some whom I had previously hated, I now most tenderly loved. Life had a new charm for me, and I remarked to my mother that it seemed that I had just begun to live. So in spite of all the doubts suggested by the evil one, I testified publicly how God had most wonderfully blessed me. While testifying, I was blessed again.

FEELINGS

I now turned my attention toward my feelings and decided that the normal experience of the Christian was to be happy and joyful constantly. My joy soon settled down into a deep, calm peace. Soon the enemy began to suggest, "Where is your joy? You must be losing out." At these times I tried to stir my emotions again by meditation and earnest prayer. However, I was not always successful; and often great distress settled over my spirit. Sometimes I would almost decide that I must be unsaved, although I also had victory over the sins that formerly held me in bondage, and my supreme desire was to do God's will in all things. Yet my feelings were so variable that perhaps one day I would feel glad and joyful and would conclude that I was truly saved. At such times I would decide never to doubt my experience again; then probably the next day, if not the very same day, my feelings would change, and the old doubts would come back again.

SEVERE TEMPTATIONS

I was also surprized in another respect. The old temptations that had seemingly left me never to return, as I had hoped, came back with renewed force. By earnest prayer, however, I obtained complete deliverance. This taught me the necessity of watching and praying.

RESTITUTION

After some time I received light on the subject of restitution. Although I had never committed any grave or serious wrongs against any one, yet I need to confess some things and to make proper restitution to certain individuals. This was very humbling to me, as I was generally considered a good boy and a model young man in the community where I was born and reared and where I still resided at the time of my restoration to the favor of God. In fact, many seemed to believe that I was a pretty good Christian at the very time I was in my backslidden condition. It, therefore, took a great deal of grace to humble myself sufficiently to make these wrongs right. However, I was always blessed in making the required restitution.

GOING TO EXTREMES

At first Satan tried to keep me from making any restitution. Then, after I had started, and he saw he could not prevent me, he pushed me to the other extreme. One little neglect or forgetfulness after another came to mind until it seemed to me there would be no end of making reparation. These little shortcomings were so trivial in their nature that, as I now review them, I am convinced that they were either no wrongs at all or else merely mistakes resulting from a lack of wisdom or knowledge, and that they had been readily overlooked at the time or soon forgotten by all parties concerned until my own mind began to search for them.

The following will suffice as a fair sample: I had by oversight forgotten to return a borrowed lead pencil, which had been about three-fourths used up. Months afterwards I happened to think of it, and I became so worried and accused that I finally attempted restitution, as I had already done in perhaps dozens of other just such trivial instances.

I was also driven to the consideration of my past conduct in the light of my present experience. I then made apologies one after another for my past failures. In some instances this was perfectly proper; but again I was driven to such extremes that I scarcely had any peace. The natural result was that I watched every word and act so carefully that often I was afraid to smile, for fear I might laugh at the wrong time. I was so busy watching myself that I did not get much enjoyment out of my religious experience. Indeed, the standard I set for myself was so rigid that I speedily came into bondage. I was unhappy myself and made others unhappy about me. However, I had no intention of going back into sin.

BECOMING ASCETIC

I took a great interest in reading religious books and papers. Although doubtless the motives of those who wrote these were high and noble, and their sole aim and purpose was to further the interests of God's kingdom on earth, yet some of these productions were written in such a manner as to cause a conscientious soul to feel that it is almost impossible for an ordinary person to reach a standard of experience and life such as they set up. My natural tendency, however, impelled me to try in my weak way to pattern after the most rigid examples. I noticed that some of the characters mentioned were given to much fasting and to abstinence from all except the very plainest of foods. My tendency toward extremes again asserted itself, and sometimes I felt condemned for enjoying even a wholesome meal. I remember one occasion when I worried because I had indulged in eating a reasonable amount of meat which was pleasing to my taste.

The last year I was in school these morbid tendencies reached their climax. I had read of devoted men in the ministry who had labored so zealously that they allowed themselves only six hours sleep. Besides their daily tasks, which were enormous, some of these men had spent as long as two hours each day in private devotions. I tried to force myself to this rigid routine, besides keeping up with my classes in the university. Almost every night religious services were held either in the chapel or in some cottage. On Sunday there were four and sometimes five services. Of course, I felt duty bound to attend all of these, besides keeping up daily my two hours of private devotions. Sometimes I was obliged to lose a part of the six hours allotted for sleep, in order to carry out this rigid program I had set for myself. Not only did I suffer from exhaustion induced by the constant and heavy strain; but if I happened to fail in spending the full two hours in prayer or in reading the Scriptures, I would sometimes be so terribly accused that I would resort to a public confession of my "neglect," and once I went to the public altar under accusation that was largely due to this very cause.

I had heard a great deal, also, concerning our obligation to do personal work and threw myself into this phase of Christian activity. Of course, I soon went to extremes. If I happened to be in the company of some one for a short time and failed to speak to him about his soul's welfare, I was likely to be dreadfully accused for gross neglect of duty. Under such circumstances it was hard for me to testify, because the accuser could always find some "neglect" or "oversight" with which to trouble me. On the other hand, I was afraid not to testify lest I should soon be hopelessly backslidden if I neglected this duty. So I finally drifted into the habit of silently asking God's forgiveness for any possible "neglect" in any way, just before rising to testify, so as to make sure that I was in a proper condition to witness for the Lord. All this was exceedingly wearing on my whole being.

A MORBID CONSCIENCE

At last my conscience became so morbid that every sermon I heard and every religious book or tract I read was at once compared with my experience to see if I lacked in even the lightest details. I happened to read of one devoted man who literally gave all his possessions to the Lord's work. Immediately I thought of the small amount of money that I had with which to pay my winter's tuition in the university.

It was not quite enough to pay all my expenses, and yet when I would decide that I could not give my "all" to the Lord's work, terrible accusations would crush me down until it seemed that my reason itself would become unbalanced. In my despair, I opened up my heart to a trusted friend, and he showed me that this was clearly an accusation from Satan and should be entirely ignored. All these things told sadly on my mental and physical condition, so that when the school year ended and I returned home to my friends, they were very much disappointed in me. Finally they became alarmed at my morbid condition.

OBTAINING RELIEF

Satan at last overdid himself; and by the help of kind friends, I discerned his devices and the extremes to which I had been driven. Once the following lines were quoted to me: "If you want to be distracted, look about you; if you would be miserable, look within; but if you would be happy, look to Jesus." These I shall never forget. A friend also pointed out the fact that I was constantly feeling my spiritual pulse. He said that this was just as detrimental to my spiritual condition as the constant counting of heart-beats would be to my physical health. Just as a patient would be likely to imagine himself afflicted with heart-trouble, so the same habit in the spiritual realm would, if continually indulged, prove disastrous to constant peace and victory.

It took some time to throw off entirely the "straight jacket" which had been imposed upon me; but by patient persistence, with God's grace, I was made an overcomer. I was taught to discern the difference between accusations and the workings of the Spirit of God. The voice of the accuser is harsh, cruel, nagging, or exacting; God's Spirit is mild, gentle, and encouraging. When God's Spirit reveals anything, it is made clear and plain. The accuser bewilders, confuses, and discourages. I also learned that our kind heavenly Father is not watching for an opportunity to cast us off, but rather he is seeking by the wooings of his gentle Spirit to lead us into green pastures and beside the still waters, where we may nourish our souls and become strong to meet the battles and trials of life. He will show us our shortcomings, but not in a way that will discourage or crush us.

Oftentimes while I was under such crushing accusations, the tempter would say, "How can you ever hope to preach the gospel, when you are so unsettled in your own experience?" One day there came to my mind the scripture in Eph. 3:20, which says that he is able to do exceeding abundantly above all that we can ask or think. I decided that in some way God would work out his purpose concerning my life if I would patiently serve him to the best of my knowledge and ability.

INHERITED DISPOSITION TO WORRY

Another lesson I needed to learn was to trust God with the future. I was naturally inclined to worry. For several generations back my ancestors on one side of my family tree had been given to excessive worry, their condition at times bordering on utter despondency. I was painfully conscious of this inheritance in my constitutional make-up. In my morbid imagination, nearly every threatening trouble was magnified to the proportion of a dreadful disaster.

Many an hour, and even days, I wasted in useless worry. Perhaps not one tenth of my gloomy forebodings ever materialized.

FACING A NERVOUS COLLAPSE

In order to teach me more thoroughly the lesson of trust, the Lord permitted me to pass through a peculiar and severe trial. As I looked forward to the time when I hoped to take up the active work of the ministry, I had a great desire to be at my best in every way. I had hoped to be in good health so that I might be able to bear the strain of the work and to meet every emergency that might arise. But just as I was about ready to enter upon my life's mission, I found my health breaking and myself on the verge of a nervous breakdown. This was indeed a keen disappointment to me. My sufferings at times seemed almost intolerable. I could not understand it: I longed so much to be of real service to God and to accomplish what I regarded as my life-work—the ministry.

Although the prospects seemed gloomy and my friends expected a complete breakdown in my health, yet I determined to go forward in the name of the Lord and to do the best I could. I even began to fear that my reason would be dethroned. However, I said nothing about my condition to my congregation, but sought to be a blessing to them in every way. I finally tried to form the habit of beginning each day with a season of thanksgiving for all the blessings I could think of. This proved to be very helpful.

RELIEVED BY HELPING OTHERS

Some days were more trying than others. While passing through the severest tests I learned that it was very helpful to look for some other tried or tempted ones and do my best to cheer and comfort them. Just a few doors from where I roomed was a lady past middle age, who had been a sufferer for eleven years. She had been helpless during the greater part of that time. I went to see her often and did what I could to lighten her burdens. She knew nothing of my sufferings, however. She was so grateful for everything I did for her, and the Lord's presence was so real every time I talked or prayed with her that invariably I was abundantly helped in the very efforts put forth to cheer and comfort her. Sometimes my heart carried an almost intolerable burden; but after a call in this home of affliction, my burden would grow light and I would sometimes wonder which had been helped the more, she or I. Also, when I considered what she had endured for so long, I was ashamed to tolerate anything like discontent concerning my own lot, which, though seemingly so hard at times, was so much better and easier, in some respects at least, than hers.

There were times when, to add to my sufferings, Satan would bring against me accusations that I could not have borne without special help from God. Often the old temptations to doubt my experience of salvation would return with tremendous force, and if I had listened to the enemy's suggestions, I should have cast aside my experience in spite of all that God had ever done for me. The accuser would sometimes begin by suggesting that I had never been truly sanctified. (I obtained the experience of entire sanctification soon after entering the work of the ministry.) Then the enemy would become more bold and would suggest, "You know that you have often had serious doubts concerning your experience of justification, and after all, perhaps you have never been truly converted."

After annoying and distressing me in this manner, Satan would fling at me such taunts as these: "You are a pretty example of a minister who is supposed to be truly called and qualified of God to preach his Word." Many times I would have a conflict like this just before rising to preach. If I had given way to feelings, I would rather have sought some place of quiet seclusion than to have faced the waiting congregation before me. But then the thought would come, "Perhaps in the congregation there are tempted and tried souls who need special help"; and so I would decide to preach, not according to how I felt, but according to actual knowledge of God's Word, which is ever unchanging. It seemed that whenever I was most severely tried in this manner, I would get the greatest victory and blessing by moving out in the performance of whatever duty confronted me. Indeed, I do not remember a single instance when I failed to preach at the appointed hour on account of the state of my feelings.

I sometimes wondered why the conflict was so long, for I suffered thus month after month. Sometimes I comforted myself with the thought that some day death would bring relief; but I learned at last that God was only permitting these sufferings in order to refine the gold. My best and most helpful sermons were preached while I was in the very midst of the deepest suffering.

BECOMING RECONCILED

At last I came to realize that it mattered not so much, after all, how much I suffered, just so the people whom I served were helped and blessed; that true blessedness in life does not consist in freedom from suffering, but in accomplishing one's mission in the world according to the divine plan.

CHRIST MORE REAL

Some of my most precious seasons of fellowship with Christ were experienced, when, in the absence of all feeling, except that of severe suffering, I would say by faith alone, "Thou, O Christ, art by my side. Thou wilt never leave me nor forsake me." At last I accustomed myself to believe his presence was real in spite of my feelings, so that by faith I could almost imagine him at my side. As I walked, it seemed that we kept step together; as I faced my congregations, he stood by my side, unseen of course by physical eyes, but under such circumstances the natural eyes can not be compared with the spiritual sight for clearness of vision. I then learned what Paul meant to express when he said, "While we look not at the things which are seen, but at the things which are not seen: for the things which are seen are temporal; but the things which are not seen are eternal" (2 Cor. 4:18). "Whom having not seen, ye love; in whom, though now ye see him not, yet believing, ye rejoice with joy unspeakable and full of glory" (1 Pet. 1:8).

SOME LESSONS LEARNED

Thus my trials and hardships taught me that a genuine
experience of salvation is obtained, as well as maintained,
not by working up some great feeling or emotion, but by
simple, trusting faith in God, and implicit obedience to his
Word.

I found that our God is a loving Father and not a hard
taskmaster. "Like as a father pitieth his children, so the
Lord pitieth them that fear him" (Psa. 103:13). Neither does
he require us to do anything that is unreasonable. "I
beseech you, therefore, brethren, by the mercies of God,
that ye present your bodies a living sacrifice, holy,
acceptable unto God, which is your reasonable service"
(Rom. 12:1).

I also learned that the true test of our Christian experience
is not the state of our feelings, but the power to resist
temptation, to keep sweet under severe trials, and to
manifest the meek and gentle spirit of the Master. I learned,
moreover, that the Lord is not anxious to cast us off for
every little failure, but is long-suffering and patient with us
as long as we have a sincere aim and purpose to please him
in all things. I learned more fully the secret of "casting all
my care upon him," knowing that "all things work together
for good to them that love God" (Rom. 8:28).

The last few years of my life have been marked by great
victory in my experience. The former trials through which I
passed have increased my usefulness by helping me to be
more unselfish. I wondered at the time why God permitted
such trials and sufferings; but now as I look back upon the
past, I see that I could not afford to be without the
discipline and training which those severe trials brought to

me. In my work as a pastor I am all the more qualified to sympathize with and to help those who are meeting with similar trials and difficulties. As I remember my own conflicts and trials, I can be more charitable for others.

CONCLUSION

As the Lord turned again the captivity of Job and restored to him his former blessings, so he restored my health in due time, together with great victory along every line. Though I still meet with hard trials and perplexing problems, yet I have learned to take them all to him in simple, trusting faith, fully assured that he will direct in all things. As already explained, my natural tendency was to worry; yet through God's grace I have been able to meet some of the most perplexing problems with calmness and even in the face of these things to enjoy refreshing sleep, knowing that "he is able to do exceeding abundantly above all that we ask or think" (Eph. 3:20).

I have ceased to long for an experience like that of some one else, knowing that God has given me one that is best for me. Peter and John were both true disciples of our Lord, yet how differently did they manifest outwardly the workings of God's Spirit within, which is ever the same!

Some years ago I discerned the oneness of God's people and became fully convinced that the Word of God should be our guide in all things pertaining to our spiritual welfare; that none of it should be omitted or cast aside. Since that time the light has been constantly increasing, and each succeeding year becomes more blessed in his service. I am learning more and more, as Paul expresses it, that "in whatsoever state I am, therewith to be content" (Phil. 4:11). With the past all under the blood, I have no gloomy forebodings concerning the future; "for I know whom I have believed, and am persuaded that he is able to keep that which I have committed unto him against that day" (2 Tim. 1:12).

The Testimony of a Prisoner

EXPERIENCE NUMBER 3

"The heart is deceitful above all things, and is desperately wicked" (Jer. 17:9). The truthfulness of this scripture has been verified in my life. For more than twenty years I lived a most shameful life to satisfy the desires of my wicked heart. I have learned that the more a person yields to the sinful desires of the heart, the more wicked he becomes.

Many times during my early school days I yielded to the tempter and played truant and ofttimes concluded that it was too hot to study and yielded to the suggestion to go for a swim in the pond, regardless of consequences. After playing truant the first time, I found a repetition of the act much easier, until finally my parents became disgusted with me and sent me away to work, and I have worked ever since that time. While in the coal-mines, I received many hard knocks and bumps, and my education neglected; whereas, had I not yielded to my wilfulness and the deceitful desires of my heart in the beginning, I might have had a splendid education and today be the possessor of a responsible position.

On my fifteenth birthday I took my first drink, yielding to the temptation of taking my dinner-pail and getting ten cents' worth of beer to drink beneath a shady tree. Oh, that God would have taken me before it ever touched my lips! I am unable to relate all my experiences since I took my first drink, but would say that I have suffered beyond measure and have paid a great price for my folly. It has robbed me of my character, reputation, friends, a beloved wife, and four beautiful children—three boys and a girl—whom I loved more than my own life.

After drink had robbed me of all that was dear to my heart, then the suggestion came for still further destruction by committing suicide. The evil one suggested that as there was nothing left worthy a continuation of my life, it were better to end it all and find sweet rest in the grave. I was cast into prison, and the way before me truly seemed dark.

While I was serving a prison sentence I learned there was help for me through the salvation of Jesus Christ. It was in the Bible that I learned that the Lord would create within me a new heart if I would only let him in, and "old things are passed away; behold, all things are become new." I thought that I was too far gone to be forgiven, but the words found in Isa. 1:18 gave me assurance: "Though your sins be as scarlet, they shall be white as snow: though they be red like crimson, they shall be as wool." These words were to me what a life-preserver is to a drowning person. I grasped them with a trembling heart and found peace to my soul.

Now, instead of destroying my own life by committing suicide and seeking rest in the grave, as Satan had often suggested, I found sweet rest to my soul in turning to Jesus, and the most earnest desire of my heart is to serve him and do that which is pleasing in his sight. Now it is a pleasant pastime, a joy and pleasure, to read the Bible and religious books, tracts, and papers, whereby I can learn more of the beauties of a life of salvation. May God help sinners everywhere to seek him while he may be found.

A Little Chinese Girl

EXPERIENCE NUMBER 4

She was only a little Chinese girl, like ten thousand of others in the great heathen land of which she was a native. She was the youngest of three children, and her father died while she was but a babe. The mother, being left a poor widow, was unable to support her little family. Therefore, according to Chinese custom, the son (who was the oldest of the three) was to receive the mother's attention, but the two daughters were to be sold into other homes, to become wives as soon as they were of marriageable age.

It is about the baby girl, Baulin, of whom I wish to tell you in this story. The case was put into her grandfather's hands for management, who arranged for her to go into her uncle's home, and to finally become the wife of her cousin, who was a little younger than herself. As soon as she was a few years old she was trained to help wash the clothes, cook the family rice, and clean the bowls; and at an early age she had to work many long hours in a silk-factory for only a few cents a day. These few cents helped to buy her own rice, and as her uncle was a poor man, he could not afford to support his "si-fu" (daughter-in-law) without receiving something for it. Never a day was this dear child sent to school. It was not customary to educate Chinese girls, except it should be those of greater wealth or rank.

Time went on until Baulin was about fourteen years old. In the meantime her uncle had come in contact with missionaries representing the full gospel of Jesus Christ. As he became better acquainted with the doctrine, and obtained an experience of salvation, he saw that it would not be right to enforce the marriage of Baulin to his son; the matter was to be left to their own choice, when they grew old enough to decide. Still the responsibility was upon him to continue supporting her to the same extent that he previously had.

In the course of another year or two, Baulin not only had shown an interest in the gospel, but had a desire to take up her abode in the mission compound to assist with the cooking for the other natives who lived there. In this capacity she faithfully labored a few months, during which time she came for prayer for salvation. The missionaries in charge had found difficulty in obtaining native help for their own kitchen. One day it suddenly dawned upon the mistress of the house that Baulin might be trained for the culinary department. When the idea was suggested, this dear young girl was delighted at the thought of promotion in usefulness. Arrangements were immediately made, and the new plan proved successful. Though she did not so much as know how to pare potatoes, fry eggs, nor set the table for foreign food, yet her eager willingness to learn made her easy to teach. Her natural inability to take responsibility, to manage, and to exercise her own judgment, were points greatly against her becoming a competent cook. However, by the mistress continuing to plan the meals and to bear the general responsibility,

Baulin soon developed into a very reliable and useful worker.

Two years later when the missionaries moved to another station, she was pleased to accompany them and to continue as their cook. In the meantime, however, a serious change came over her uncle, which made Baulin entertain fears concerning her former engagement for marriage. This man, who was so dependable before, gradually became entangled in business matters, swindled others out of a considerable amount of money, resulting in his utter spiritual downfall. Instead of making efforts to rise again, he seemed to sink deeper and deeper into sin, until all hope was given up for his return. Baulin was exceedingly fond of her own people, and her relatives were not a few. But after her uncle had backslidden, she began to receive more or less persecution from her people. It so happened that the new station to which she accompanied the new missionaries was the city in which her mother lived. She was employed there as servant for a high-class family. The mother, though having been in contact with the Christian religion for many years, still remained a rank heathen, having great faith in the worship of idols. The time came when the missionaries were about to depart on furlough to the homeland, and now a serious question confronted Baulin: "What shall I do, or what can I do?"

But before continuing this narrative, let me say here that during the three years that she was employed as cook, she made a perfect record of honesty and uprightness— something which probably can not be said of one out of a hundred of Chinese cooks. Not once was she even suspected of taking without permission, so much as a crust of bread or a spoonful of anything belonging to the foreign kitchen. When other natives of the compound would ask her for a bit of food which happened to be left in the dishes, she would never give it without first asking permission to do so. She seldom broke dishes, but when she did, she lost no time in making acknowledgment. Thus her honesty, conscientiousness, and modesty won a warm place in the hearts of those whom she served, and when she appealed to them for help in solving the problem which so perplexed her mind about the time that she must be separated from them, they gladly shared her burden. It was by seeing her stedfastness through this trial that her real worth could be appreciated more than ever before.

From a Chinese point of view, she was still under age, though she was now about eighteen. Her mother had never given up the idea that she should be married to her cousin when they both became old enough. At this time her uncle was in a backslidden state, and in all probability would insist on the marriage. The boy himself, her cousin, was growing up rather a worthless young man. He had been in school more or less, but was not extra bright. Recently his father had placed him as an apprentice in a shoeshop. He had shown no inclination whatsoever toward spiritual things, though he had had many advantages of hearing the gospel. Baulin knew that she would soon be out of employment, and this meant much to the young girl; for she was now fully self-supporting and, besides, had helped her uncle more than once in his financial straits. To return to the former mission station, at which city most of her people lived, seemed the only open door before her. Yet this meant more persecution, and should she have to return to the silk-factory to work, she would be deprived of attending meeting, for the girls and women employed there must toil on from early morn till late at night, seven days a week.

It was when she heard that her uncle was making a business trip to the city where she was now living and where her mother also lived, that she became more anxious concerning a quick settlement of that marriage question, and it was in this that she earnestly begged the missionary to help. A meeting was called at which Baulin, her mother, her uncle, the missionary, and a few others were present. Baulin requested a written agreement signed by her mother and uncle, that the engagement to her cousin was broken, and that they should have no power to compel her engagement to any one else, but that she should have the right herself to make choice of her life companion. The question was discussed, but met with extreme opposition at first by the mother, insomuch that the girl finally declared that because she was a Christian and desired to do the right she would die rather than be compelled to marry a man who was not a Christian and one whom she did not love. The uncle's greatest objection was that he had no money to buy another girl for his son, and the son would blame his father for not having a wife ready for him, according to Chinese custom.

After several meetings, hours of discussion, and much prayer on the part of the Christians, a paper and a duplicate were finally signed, which set this dear young Christian free from her childhood engagement, and oh, what a beaming countenance she wore! Keenly did she realize it would not be easy to return to her home city and face her heathen relatives, who would all be against her on account of the step she had taken, but she was very happy in knowing that her persecution was for righteousness' sake. Well able did she feel, through the grace of God, to meet the worst that might come.

Her joy was increased some days later, when word was received that the mission station in the same city where her people lived would be glad to use her as cook and general helper in the house. Thus she would not need to go back to the factory to earn a living, but could be employed more directly in the service of God and be under the care of the church.

I hope all who read this true story will not forget to breathe a prayer for this dear young girl, who so boldly took her stand for the truth and right, in the midst of opposition from heathen relatives. We can not but hope that she may some day be as reliable a spiritual worker as she is today a temporal worker.

Persecutions and Victories of an Evangelist

EXPERIENCE NUMBER 5

It is with pleasure and gratitude that I take advantage of this opportunity of telling of God's wonderful dealings with me. It is now a little over ten years since I was converted. I had the advantage of being reared in a Christian home. My parents having been saved for a good many years.

When I first heard of people who believed the entire Word of God as it was preached in the days of the apostles, I wondered what kind of people they were. Some of the ministers were conducting some meetings not far from where we lived, and, hearing of these people, I asked my father if it would not be possible for them to come to our community. Being surprized at my question and glad to hear that I was interested in hearing those people, he suggested that I should speak to them personally and ask them to come. These meetings were conducted about eight miles from our home.

It was a cold October day when I drove to the place with horse and buggy and asked the people to come to our town. They were glad for the invitation, and we returned to my home the same day. There was especially one thing about them which surprized me, and that was how happy and contented they seemed to be; but I was a little unwilling to believe that it was really possible for a person to enjoy religion, for my association with so-called Christian people had made the impression upon my mind that Christianity, or salvation, was only for those who could not enjoy themselves in the world.

When the company that were to hold the meeting came to our home, I decided to study and examine their lives to find out whether they really possessed the joy and satisfaction that I was longing for. Their quiet, devoted lives convinced me of the fact that I ought to become a Christian. Deep conviction settled down upon me in the meetings. My mother and father, whose lives had made a deep impression upon me, pleaded with me to yield to God, but I was still unwilling to surrender.

After the meetings closed I tried to quench the Spirit by indulging in worldly pleasures and associating with my old friends, but it seemed that the Spirit of God was working so powerfully upon me that it was impossible to resist him. I remember especially an experience one afternoon. I was brought face to face with the supreme question, Are you ready to meet God? I decided that I would not yield, but that I would enjoy the pleasure of sin and the world for some years and later become a Christian.

Not being able to quench the convictions that the Spirit of God had wrought upon me, I deliberately indulged in blasphemy, determined to make the Holy Spirit leave me, but I am glad to say that God was merciful to me in not permitting my soul to be lost. For a moment I felt as though I had committed the unpardonable sin, that heaven was closed, and that my soul was lost forever. But I turned to God with tears and a broken heart, the Spirit of God again strove with me, and my sins were mercifully forgiven. The joy of heaven filled my soul, and I received the assurance that my name was written in the Book of Life. This was November 5, 1905.

SANCTIFICATION

My soul was perfectly satisfied, and for some time I felt as though all that heaven could give to a human being in this world had been given to me. But later I began to realize the need of something more. I heard teaching on the doctrine of entire sanctification and began to study about it in the Bible. The knowledge thus obtained caused me to seek for the experience, but I did not receive it as soon as I had expected. After some very hard struggles and much disappointment I finally concluded that the teaching was wrong in regard to this matter and that it was impossible to obtain the experience as it had been presented to me. Trying to comfort myself with this thought, I let the matter rest for a while, but I was not satisfied.

About two years after my conversion I decided that this matter should be settled between God and my soul. Going to the Lord in earnest prayer, I made a perfect consecration of all to God. The Lord began talking to my soul, and he made it clear to me that the reason why I had not obtained the experience sooner was not because the doctrine I had heard was wrong, but because I had an exaggerated idea of what sanctification really would do. I was under the impression that everything in my human nature which had caused me trouble would be removed in sanctification. I had failed to see that in sanctification human desires are not taken away but sanctified. I saw clearly that the cause for the most of my troubles was that I had failed to discriminate between carnality and humanity.

While I was consecrating, the Lord spoke to me, not audibly but by his Spirit, and asked me if I was willing to go to Denmark with the gospel. I was able to surrender on all points but this one, seeing that going to a foreign country would conflict with all my plans for the future. I felt very much like Abraham when he went to Mount Moriah with his only son to offer him there upon God's altar. But seeing that this was the only way and desiring to obtain the experience, I surrendered, placed all on the altar, and immediately I was sanctified and baptized with the Holy Ghost. Praise the Lord!

There were no outward demonstrations, no special manifestations of the power of God; but the Holy Ghost, being enthroned in my heart, gave me a power over the world and self which I had not experienced heretofore. This glorious experience I have now enjoyed for several years, and it never was more precious to me than it is at the present time. Halleluiah!

GOING TO A FOREIGN COUNTRY

For a while I did not think more about my call to the work
of God in Europe, but there was a deep longing in my soul
to see people saved, and whenever time permitted I would
do all the personal work I could, distributing literature,
visiting people in their homes, helping in meetings, etc.

My parents being Danish, they naturally made me think
more of the Scandinavian people than I otherwise would
have thought, and my heart was often burdened that this
glorious truth might be brought to them. These thoughts I
kept to myself, speaking only to God about the matter. At
last the burden became so heavy that I opened my heart to a
minister in whom I had very much confidence, and he told
me that a year before that time the Lord had clearly shown
that I should go to Denmark with the gospel.

Next I opened my heart to my parents. Naturally they felt
sorry that I should leave them, but in another sense they
were glad to see me enter the work of the Lord. The Lord
had revealed to my mother the evening of my conversion
that I should preach the gospel, but she did not think that
my field of labor would be in a foreign country.

An older minister, who had for some time been thinking of
going to Scandinavia, asked me if it would not be possible
for me to accompany him; and when the matter was
brought before the church, it was finally decided that I
should go. We sailed from New York Dec. 18, 1909, and
arrived in Denmark, Jan. 3, 1910. This brother and his wife
stayed with relatives, while I made my home with different
people, some of them unsaved; and the most disagreeable
thing that I met at the beginning was that I was often

obliged to stay in homes where I knew I was not welcome. But in all the trials and disappointments there was one thing that especially encouraged and comforted me, and that was that I knew God had sent me to Scandinavia.

I shall never forget the first time God gave me a little favor among the people. An old gentleman expressed his desire to have me give my testimony after the sermon. I was at that time unable to express my thoughts in the Danish language, but in my heart I carried a very heavy burden for the people. With this burden on my soul I arose, and the feelings I could not express in words I expressed in tears. That evening four souls came to the altar and were gloriously saved. From that time on my services were in demand, and it was not long until a goodly number sought the Lord in the meetings.

About a year from this time a Baptist minister asked me to come to his town and hold a four days' meeting. After earnestly praying over the matter I decided to break my engagement at another place (something I do not do unless specially directed of the Lord) and to hold these meetings. Instead of holding four meetings, I held one hundred and thirty meetings, and about one hundred souls were gloriously saved. There were a number of young men in the town who determined that they would break up the meetings, but we asked them to come and take part in the song-service, which generally commenced about a half hour before the preaching-service. Often the stores would be closed early in order that the people might be able to attend the meetings, and it was not long until nearly all the young men of the town were sitting on the front seats listening to the word with tears in their eyes.

An intoxicated man, who was sent out by a saloon-keeper to make disturbance, attacked me in front of the congregation. A young man who also was under the influence of liquor but who was in sympathy with the work I was doing, stepped to my side and offered to defend me with his fist. In anger he said to the other man, "I want to tell you that we are not going to let you disturb our meetings." I tried to calm them, but in spite of all I did, the man was unmercifully treated as soon as he got outside by the people whose sympathies had been won by the gospel.

PERSECUTED FOR THE GOSPEL'S SAKE

The saloon-keeper mentioned above, who almost failed in business because of the revival, tried to work out a plot against me. He had a friend who lived in the State of Michigan, to whom he wrote for information concerning my life. This man wrote back: "The minister who is preaching in your town is a professional white-slave trader, and has escaped the authorities here in America and fled to Europe." This letter was taken to the officials in Denmark, and immediately I was arrested. One of the best detectives in the kingdom and several state officials were working on the case. A number of impressions were taken of my fingers and my picture was hung up in police stations among those of professional thieves and criminals.

A very bitter persecution also broke out in the Scandinavian press. Among the people I was generally known as "The Prophet." My aunt and cousin in Copenhagen were nearly dumbfounded one day, when, as they passed one of the large printing-houses in the city, they saw on the news bulletin of a prominent daily in large bold type, which could be read at a long distance, the following:

"The Prophet Morris Johnson—White-Slave Trader—Baptized Naked Women—Stole Church's Money-Box—Went to America with Fifty Young Girls and Sold Them to the Houses of Ill-Fame—Escaped the Hands of the Authorities."

None of these things were true, however; but wherever I went I was carefully watched by the authorities. My name was associated with the most ignoble, immoral, and dishonorable things, and the matter was given such publicity that I could not board a train or a steamer without its being made known to those around me.

Finally the people of God to whom I had been preaching considered it their duty to encourage me to appeal to the law for protection, one brother offering to spend five thousand crowns on the case. This I could not do, for it would have conflicted with my Christian principles; but at last I saw that the only way I could satisfy them was to do something to prove that I was not guilty of the accusations.

Accordingly I went to Copenhagen, spoke to the United States Minister and to a prominent lawyer about the matter. They encouraged me to take up a law suit against the parties who had so inhumanly treated me, but feeling that I should grieve God by doing so, I decided to patiently suffer, knowing that God would stand by me and that in the end his name would be glorified. I must admit that had it not been for the fact that the people of God were praying for me and that God in a special way comforted and strengthened me, I should not have been able to stand through this trial.

About three months after the time I had been in Copenhagen, a state official published in the paper an article in which he made known to the public that after a thorough examination of my case they were satisfied that I was innocent and was worthy of the moral support of the people.

REVIVALS

I am glad to say that this persecution resulted in a wonderful outbreak of spiritual life in Scandinavia. Hundreds of people came out to the meetings and a large number of souls were saved. The State Bishop, a very influential man, was called upon to oppose the meetings. In a public discourse he mentioned my name twenty times, but this only aroused a greater curiosity in the hearts of the people to hear the word, and in this way people were brought under the influence of the gospel who would never have been reached any other way.

I shall never forget an experience I had in a revival in Hjorring, Denmark. We had rented a large hall, and the first evening there were about five hundred people present. I had been passing through some very hard trials just before this meeting, but the trial reached its climax as I stood before that audience. I did not feel the help of the Holy Spirit at all as I was preaching. I went to my room that evening with a heavy heart and spent some time on my knees in earnest prayer.

Later it was made clear to me why God permitted me to pass through this trial. The following Sunday evening the power of the Holy Spirit was poured out upon that audience in such a measure that it was almost impossible for the people to resist it. There were about 750 people present, and most of them stayed for the altar-service. There was not room at the altar for those who wanted to seek God, so the people fell on their knees and began to pray, and all over the hall one could hear sinners crying to God for mercy. Many of them were saved. The meeting did not close until after midnight. I then saw that the reason why God had permitted me to pass through that test was that he might prepare me for the great blessing presently to be poured out upon the meeting.

ALL-NIGHT MEETING

In Lokken, Denmark, the people of God gathered one evening for a special meeting. The word of God became so precious to us that we could not leave the place. A large number testified and after midnight we had an ordinance-meeting, which was followed by a sermon, and that by an altar-call. Several came forward and sought the Lord for sanctification, and a few who were so much interested that they could not leave, came and were saved. The altar-service was broken up when a brother came in and exclaimed, "Hurry up, or you'll miss the train." This was the morning train, which left at five o'clock. The good work continued at this place, and there were open doors for me to preach the gospel in all parts of the kingdom where before warnings had been published against me.

MEETING A PHILOSOPHER

During my stay in Copenhagen it was my privilege to become acquainted with an educated young man, a doctor of philosophy, who had been influenced by higher critics, such as have doubted the miraculous accounts given in the Holy Scriptures. When I was introduced to him, I noticed that he thought it would not be very difficult for him to weaken my faith and confidence in regard to religious matters. He immediately expressed his desire to have some private talks on religious questions, to which I gladly consented, but greatly feeling my need of special wisdom and grace from God. We would often sit up until after midnight, but I enjoyed these conversations and discussions, for they gave me an understanding of the position that such persons generally take in regard to religion.

One evening he accompanied me to the country, where I held a meeting in a private home. About fifteen minutes after I had entered the pulpit, I noticed that a deep conviction settled down upon him. Tears filled his eyes, and he was unable to hide his emotions. One night at one-thirty in the morning he said to me: "I have a question I want to ask you. I have had your life under my microscope for a while and have come to the conclusion that you are one of the happiest and most contented young men I have ever met. Still I have noticed that you have no interest whatever in the enjoyments and pleasures that other young men of your age seem to be so taken up with. Tell me, what is the source of your happiness?" My reply was, "The source of my joy and happiness is the Christ that you are trying to deny." Tears filled his eyes, and he said to me, "In my public lectures and discourses and with my pen I have tried to influence people against Christianity, but now I have found that Christianity can satisfy and make happy; so I will never use my influence in that way any more." I did not have the privilege of seeing this young man converted, but I am sure that some day I shall meet him in heaven.

TRUSTING THE LORD

When I entered the gospel field, I decided that I should trust God to supply all my needs. My father upon bidding me good-by said, "Now, my son, if you ever need help financially, you must let me know, and I shall be glad to help you." I thanked my father, but told him that he should not feel under obligations to me more than to any other missionary and that it was my intention to trust God.

I paid my own fare to Europe with the exception of one dollar, which was given me by a kind brother. For a while I got along well, for I had a little personal money; but the time came when I needed help. I especially remember one occasion when I needed some means. I prayed and wept before the Lord as a child before its father, asking the Lord what he was going to do with me now. After I had prayed a while, the Lord assured me that my prayer was heard. Two days later I received a money-order from a brother in South Dakota and was able to meet all my obligations and even had some to spare. Praise the Lord!

Another time during my stay in Norway I needed a certain amount of money and began to pray to God concerning the matter. The amount needed was about twenty dollars. A few days from that time I received a money-order for eleven dollars from some one in Copenhagen from whom it would have been altogether unreasonable for me to expect financial help. But this person wrote that God had made it clear that this money should be sent to me. I also received a letter from a man in America with a money-order for ten dollars. He wrote: "I am sending you ten dollars, and feel that I must send it off immediately. Hope you will receive it in time." My needs were supplied, and you can be sure I was a happy man. I have learned by experience that there is no life happier or nobler than the life that is fully surrendered and consecrated to God.

The Secret of a Perfect Life

EXPERIENCE NUMBER 6

A little more than half a century ago I drew my first breath of life. It was a day in early May, so I have been told: the sun was shining, the birds were singing, and the early flowers were in bloom. It is not to be supposed that my environment in life's early hour had any influence upon the passions of my soul; nevertheless, from my earliest recollection I have been an ardent lover of the esthetical in nature. Many of the days of my childhood were spent wandering through the fields in the bright sunshine, admiring and culling the flowers; rambling through the leafy wood, listening with glad heart to the songs of birds; or sitting on the mossy bank of the rippling brooklet delighted by the music made by its crystal waters as they played among the rocks.

But the happy, innocent days of childhood do not last always: the sun does not always shine, nor the birds sing; neither do the flowers always bloom along our way. Oh, if we could only have been overlooked—many of us have thought in the dreary days of after-life—by Father Time and been left behind to be always in the green, sun-lit fields of childhood, how happy we should have been! But it was not so; and now, since I have found the riches of grace, I am glad it was not so. No one can escape the onward-leading hand of Time. He will lead us, despite our protests, into days where the sun has ceased shining, where the birds have flown to a more genial clime, and where the flowers have faded. As our much-loved poet has said,

"Into each life some rain must fall—

Some days must be dark and dreary."

My life has been a confirmation of these words.

MY FIRST SIN

Among the recollections of my early childhood, one is more deeply impressed on my mind than any other, so deeply and firmly stamped that the many and varied experiences of fifty years have failed to make it less clear and distinct to the vision of memory than it was the day it occurred. It was the committing of a sin. It may have been my first wilful transgression, but, however that may be, it was one that caused an awful sense of guilt to come into my heart, and I trembled, as it were, in an unseen presence. No one had ever spoken to me of God, of shunning the wrong, or of doing the right, except my mother (sweet today is my memory of her); so I carried my trouble to her, and in her presence the tempter led me into falsehood, so that I was made more wretched than before.

GETTING DEEPER INTO SIN

The days sped on; and after a few years, I had won the title of "Bad Boy." Though the sins of those youthful days (over which I prefer to throw the relieving mantle of forgetfulness) were dark and deep, I did not altogether lose my love for the beautiful and the good. In those shadowy days, a ray of sunlight would now and then break through, a bird-note would be heard, and a fragrant flower would raise its drooping head. In such hours, I would get a glimpse of a better life. An unseen hand would set before me a picture of a pure life, and in my fancy I would see myself a good man. Oh, that the dreams of those youthful days were more perfectly fulfilled! but I must give praise to God for what he has wrought in me.

Many a time at the midnight hour in those youthful days, after I had left some den of vice, there would be whisperings in my soul of a higher, nobler life. As I, in my fancy, gazed down through the years, the angel of goodness would shift before me bright pictures of the different characteristics of a holy life. At this distant day, on looking back, I am surprized to note in what trueness the Holy Spirit set before me the ideal godly life.

But I must be brief, as only a few pages of this work are allotted to me in which to tell you how I found—or, rather, what I found to be—the secret of a perfect life.

MY CONVERSION

I was converted at the age of twenty-eight. A few months later, realizing the need of a deeper spiritual life, I yielded myself a living sacrifice to God, and he gave me the desire

of my heart. Bless his name! To tell you the joy of my soul
in these experiences, is immeasurably beyond the power of
my pen. The happiness of a pure life fancied in the day-
dreams of my youth were more than realized. Although I
was of a highly imaginative mind, the joy my heart found in
the riches of redeeming grace was numberless times greater
than the fancied joys pictured to my mind in my boyhood
hours.

My heart now flowed out in a gushing stream of love to
God, and my mind glowed with thoughts of him. It was the
poet Milton who said: "As to other points, what God may
have determined for me, I know now; but this I know—that
if he ever instilled an intense love of moral beauty into the
breast of any man, he has instilled it into mine. Ceres, in
the fable, pursued not her daughter with a greater keenness
of inquiry than I, day and night, the idea of perfection."
And I think the same was true of me.

Early in my religious life I became conscious that the law
of development is written in the Christian heart, and that
this law, if given full scope, will raise us year after year
into higher degrees of perfection. The Holy Spirit revealed
to me also at this time the secret of attaining to this perfect
life by a natural growth in grace day after day. In love and
humility lies the secret of a perfect and successful Christian
life. The earnestness with which we seek God is in
proportion to our love for him. Just as truly as the seven
colors are woven together in one white ray of sunlight, so
truly are the laws of a perfect life gathered up and fulfilled
in the life of those who love God. "Love is the fulfilling of
the law." No man can escape the effect of breaking a law of
love. What fragrance is to the flower, obedience is to love.
Any act of unfaithfulness to God or man sounds a false
note on the golden harp of love. He who loves truth

intensely will dwell with truth; he who loves purity of thought will think only on things that are pure. Vain thoughts will he hate. He who loves learning will seek after learning and just to that intensity of his love for it. He who loves home will dwell at home as much as possible, and home will become sweeter home. He who loves God will dwell with God, will seek after God, thereby strengthening his affection for God and daily growing into his perfection.

HUMILITY NEEDED

But love alone will not suffice; humility is needed that love may be rightly directed. If humility be lacking, love unconsciously begins to center in self. With a feeling of shame I confess that twice in my life since becoming a Christian, I have lost the ballast of humility so that love went astray. I thought to love God and be faithful; I thought that I was attaining to greater love; but to my surprize, when the Holy Spirit set my heart before me in the clear light of pure love, I found within that awful, ghastly, defiling principle of self-love.

If your soul loves the perfect life, "humble yourself under the hand of God" and "keep yourself in his love." After years of experiences and some sad failures, I have found, with a greater certainty than ever, that love ballasted by humility is the secret of a happy, holy life. I trust that during the remaining days of my life my soul shall flourish like the palm-tree, and grow strong like the cedars of Lebanon, and that I shall develop into that greater fulness of God—into a more perfect image of him.

Today I know that "God is love; and he that dwelleth in love dwelleth in God, and God in him." As my inner man is renewed day by day, to my spiritual eyes the ideal perfect life grows in loveliness. As I journey on toward the setting of life's sun, I can see farther into the beyond, catch clearer glimpses of unseen things, hear more distinctly the songs of angels, scent in greater sweetness the fragrance from the flowers that grow in that celestial land, and feel the beauty of the Lord growing upon me. I have passed through the furnace flames; but God has brought me through, and he will bring you through.

A PERFECT IDEAL

Have there been times in your life when a glowing feeling crept into your heart and you beheld a vision of ideal perfection? Oh, be "obedient to the heavenly vision," remembering this, that the secret of approach to your ideal is love and humility. Humility will keep you in the right path as love hurries you on after your ideal. Neither the rocks, the thorns, the waves, nor the furnace flames, retard the lover in his race for a perfect life when the vision is kept clear before his soul. Have you made failures? So have I—greater failures, perhaps, than any you have made or ever will make; but the God who transforms the caterpillar into the butterfly will transform you into his perfect image if you only love him intently and be submissive to all his will.

Conversion of a Young Jewish Rabbi

EXPERIENCE NUMBER 7

I was born in an orthodox Jewish family. When I was but four years of age, my parents took me to England and put me in charge of the late Rabbi Horowitz of London to fully teach me the basis of rabbinical life. At the age of seventeen years I completed my course of instruction as a fully legalized rabbi, but was too young to take the responsibilities of a district or synagog. At that time I returned to the United States and soon drifted into socialism and became a socialist orator, traveling from city to city and State to State, until I left the first principles of my rabbinical teaching.

While traveling through Canada I became acquainted with an anarchist and partly accepted his belief. I strayed so far away from my early teaching that from time to time while speaking, I would hold up my Hebrew Bible and tear it to pieces, cursing God and denying that there was a God. I really became so hardened that I almost believed in my heart that there was no God.

On the twenty-sixth day of October, 1907, I came to Chicago, and while I was speaking that night on the platform, holding the Hebrew Bible, tearing it, and ready to curse God, there came a sudden strong voice, as it were, and, to my surprize, repeated to me the following words: "They shall look upon me whom they have pierced, and they shall mourn after him as one mourneth for its only begotten, and they shall be in bitterness after him as one is in bitterness after his first-born."

While I listened to this, I thought that some one was behind the platform speaking these words. I looked behind the platform, but could find no one. When I resumed my speech, the voice came again speaking the same verse, and I became almost paralyzed for a while. After the meeting was over, as I walked toward my apartments, I heard the voice for the third time, speaking to me in stronger terms than ever. The miserable feelings came stronger and stronger. In fact, I began to look for peace to my conscience, but did not know how to find it. In this trouble of soul, no one among all the orators, Jewish rabbis, or religious people of different denominations came up to tell me how to do better nor to give me advice.

I left Chicago for New York, but could not find rest. The words of that voice never left me day or night. One night, while walking the streets of New York looking for something to comfort me, I saw a sign reading, "Men Wanted for the United States Army." At nine o'clock the next morning I went to the recruiting-station and asked for an application-blank. The man at the station thought it strange that a Jew would come to enlist, but he gave me an application-blank. I filled it out and was examined and sent to Ft. Slocum, New York, where I was sworn in for three years' faithful service for the United States Army. After I enlisted I began to look for peace; but the more I looked, the worse and more trouble came to me. In fact, persecutions from different soldiers were very bitter because I was a Jew and did not do what they were doing.

While in Ft. Slocum I contracted fever and was taken to a hospital. From Ft. Slocum I was sent to Ft. Sill, Oklahoma, where I was assigned to Battery B, First Field Artillery. There was only one Jewish man besides me amongst over three hundred Roman Catholics, and they believed in making things hot for us, so the more I looked for peace the worse misery and persecutions I found.

On Decoration Day, 1908, they were playing football, and after the game they went into the kitchen, procured large butcher knives, and came out to cut the "sheenies" up. When we saw them coming with the knives, we ran into the tailor-shop and locked ourselves in, hiding underneath mattresses between the covers. They broke the door, but through Providence they could not find us. Then for the first time since I had embraced socialism I began to think there was a God, since our lives were so spared.

On the sixth of June we went bathing in the Red River on the reservation, and the boys came and turned us head down and feet up in the water and wanted to drown us, but it seemed that through Providence I was once more saved from being destroyed by these blood-thirsty men. Upon our return, we found the tailor-shop flooded. This was reported to the commander, but no action was taken in regard to this or any other case of persecution.

We decided to desert the army after pay-day. When pay-day came, I had coming to me about $200 from the tailor-shop and $13 as pay for the month from the army, but out of the $200 I collected only about $70. That afternoon we walked to Lawton, Oklahoma, to get the train from there to St. Louis. Upon our arrival at St. Louis, the other man got a job, and I wrote to my uncle in Chicago, who sent me a ticket to come to Chicago. When I arrived there, he advised me to go to Canada and said that he would support me all the time that I was there, as they would apprehend me in the United States for a deserter.

I went to Canada, but was still in much distress. Some time later I had a desire to leave Vancouver, British Columbia, and go over the border into the State of Washington, but went under the assumed name of Friedman. While under that name I looked for a position, but could not find one; so I cabled to my parents for money and two weeks afterward I received enough money to open up a little store. I took for my next name Feldman. I opened a book-store, but within three months I lost almost $3,000. Then I left Seattle, Washington, for Tacoma under the name Gray.

Three weeks later I left Tacoma for Portland, Oregon, under the name of Grayson, where I looked up a friend of mine. He was at that time manager of the Oregon Hotel. The next morning I was more miserable than ever before and thought that I was sick. The night preceding I related to my friend all my troubles, with the exception of my being a deserter from the army.

While I was looking for a charity physician who could give me something to relieve my distress and trouble, I found a Salvation Army man and asked him if he knew of any physician who worked for charity and would give me treatment. He told me that he had a friend who was a physician and who was a lover of Jewish people. This was the first time that I ever heard that a Christian loved a Jew.

I went to the office of the doctor, whose name was Estock, and he gave me a cordial welcome. Putting his right hand on my right wrist and his left hand around my neck, he said that he loved the Jews because his Savior was a Jew and that he was glad God had sent me to his office in answer to his prayers. I was dumbfounded and unable to answer. The doctor said, "You do not need a physician for your body, but you need the Lord Jesus to heal your soul, for your trouble is with your soul, and the Lord Jesus is able to save you from your distress and troubles." He gave me a little bottle and said: "Here is a little medicine, but you do not need it. The only thing that will help you is prayer, and I will 'phone to my wife and ask her to pray for you, and I will also pray for you. This will be the only way you will get peace."

The next morning as I was offering my thanks to him he said, "Do not thank me, but thank God that he sent his only begotten Son, that through him such poor unworthy people as we should be saved through his love."

"What can this mean?" I answered. "Is there a God that will love such a man as I am?—a man who curses him? a man that stamped his Bible under his feet and fought against him? Is it true that he will love me so?"

The doctor answered, "He died for such men as you, that he might save you." He further said: "My house belongs to the Lord, and I owe everything to him. The God of Abraham and Isaac is my God, and the God of David and also the Prophets. He is my God, and he is your God, whether you want him or not; and I beg you to come with me to my house."

"It is impossible for me to go into your house," I answered, "because I do not believe that there is a God, and if there is one, I am unworthy to go into such a house."

He pleaded with me further to go, and I went with him. I lived at the doctor's house for thirty days. We had the strongest arguments on Scriptures, he trying to prove to me that Jesus is the Messiah that came to save his people from

sin. I contradicted every word of his with the Old
Testament Scriptures.

On the thirtieth day in the doctor's house I was more vile
than ever before. I got up in the morning looking for the
first chance to get even with the doctor because of his
persistence in mentioning the Lord Jesus on every
occasion. When I came down-stairs, they were ready for
breakfast. I sat at the table brewing within myself, full of
hatred, malice, and bitterness against them because of their
holding up to me the Lord Jesus as my only Savior. While
at the table I could not withhold my bitterness, and when
they read the Scriptures after the meal, I began to laugh,
mock, and curse, calling them all kinds of vile names.

While I was doing this they went down on their knees to
pray as they did every morning. Looking up to me, the
doctor said, "My friend, if you will not respect God nor
respect me as your only and personal friend in the city, for
the Lord's sake respect this house, for this house is
consecrated unto God."

These words sank deep into my heart, and I kneeled down
still with bitterness in my heart against Jesus and the
doctor. While I was down on my knees, I was cursing,
mocking at them and their Lord. The doctor prayed first,
then his wife, and then his little boy, who said, "Lord Jesus,
you have promised to save him; won't you save him?"

These words broke my heart, and I began crying, "If there
is a God, come and prove yourself." The carpet around me
was wet with the tears which I had shed in crying for God
to come and prove himself. I felt within myself a love for
the Lord Jesus and soon had a living faith that the Lord
Jesus died for me and that through his death I was saved.

After I rose from my knees, the doctor, his wife, and the little boy stood with eyes full of tears, rejoicing with me that there was power in the blood of Jesus Christ to save such a vile sinner as I was.

One hour later I left the house of the doctor to tell my friend, the manager of the hotel, that the Lord Jesus was now my Savior and that he had saved me from my sins. He took a heavy chunk of wood and hit me on my right side, nearly breaking my ribs.

I said, "May God forgive you for this and not hold it against you," while the tears were streaming down my face. This is the first time in my life that I ever said to any one, "May God bless you!" Then I said to him, "If it were only yesterday that you had done this to me, I would have killed you; but now the Lord Jesus has taken anger out of my heart, and I will endeavor to pray for you that God may have mercy upon you." Walking out of his hotel crippled as I was and holding my side with my hand, I said again, "God bless you!"

While walking down the street, I saw a company of mission workers on the corner of Jefferson and Washington Avenues. I pushed myself through the crowd, seeing that there were some Jews there, and I began to preach to my own people for the first time that the only way of salvation is through the Lord Jesus Christ. In answer, there came rotten eggs and rotten tomatoes at my head and body until I was covered from head to foot.

After the meeting I walked on singing a song and rejoicing that the Lord Jesus had seen fit to save such a poor sinner as I was. Thus ended my first day as a convert. I thank God for the first pay I ever received in the gospel—a crippled side and rotten eggs. I continued to preach the gospel to my people in Portland for several days.

Three days after my conversion, while I was on my knees praying, it occurred to me that I had better write to my relatives and tell them what love the Lord Jesus had for me, and that he had died to save them as well as me, and that he was the only true Messiah. I reasoned for several days against this; but at last I had to write, because I saw that the Lord was on one side and my relatives on the other side, and that I had to choose between them. So I wrote to them, sending to each a separate letter telling them that Jesus was my Savior and that he is the only and true Messiah.

Sometime after this, answer came from my relatives that they could not believe that there was any power to save me, because, if I could leave my first principles and leave my own people, the teaching which I was brought up under and drift so far away as to curse God, they did not believe there was any power to save me. I kept sending them Testaments and Gospels, but still they could not believe.

One day I went to see my sister and told her the truth. She at first did not believe me, but I asked her to attend a street-meeting which I was to hold, and she heard me preach Christ. She then wrote to my mother, who began to grieve herself to death because I had accepted the Lord Jesus for my Savior. Then they wrote me different letters and were patient with me, thinking that they would win me back to Judaism. When they saw there was no hope of getting me back, they were done with me.

On one occasion while standing in the street and preaching, there came a thought to me with great force, "If the authorities get you for a deserter, what will you do?" This question troubled me so that I could not continue my meetings. I went to the doctor's office and said to him, "Dr. Estock, do you know what they do to a person that has deserted the United States Army?"

"They give him three or four years in the military penitentiary," he answered.

"Do you know that I am a deserter from the United States Army?"

He looked at me puzzled and said, "How can this be?"

"It is true, and I must give myself up to the army authorities before they get me and disgrace my belief in the Lord Jesus."

I proposed giving myself up the next day, but the doctor told me to be in no haste and said he would ask several people of God to pray for me to learn what the mind of God was before I took another step. After a few days they came to the conclusion that they would send me to Canada, where I should be out of the jurisdiction of the United States and should be free. Thinking that this offer was of the Lord, I accepted it and left for Toronto, Canada. Upon my arrival at Toronto I felt the Lord speaking to me and saying, "The more you run away from my law, the more miserable you will feel. Go back to the United States."

This was while I was in the hotel at night and could not sleep. I felt very miserable to know that the step I had taken in coming to Toronto was not God's will and in his order. I had only $3.10 in my possession. In the morning I went to the ticket-office to inquire how much it cost to go to Buffalo. They told me it would cost $3.10. I then purchased a ticket for Buffalo. When I arrived I telegraphed to the doctor, stating that I was glad that I had come back to the United States to give myself up to the army authorities. The doctor replied by telegraph, stating that I was out of God's will and order in coming back to the United States to give myself up, and that therefore he could not have fellowship with me any more. Bitterly weeping over the message, I said to myself, "Now the only friend I have is gone." But this promise encouraged me, that my God would never turn against me nor forsake me. There I was, left without a friend and without money in my pockets to procure a night's lodging.

As it was bitterly cold, I prayed to the Lord that he would send somebody along that would take me home with him. As I was praying, a man passed by, and I asked him if he knew whether there was any child of God in the city. He said a woman who was his neighbor was a child of God, and he took me to her home. It was true that she was a child of God and her home a godly one.

Soon after this I went to Pittsburg, and the Lord opened up the hearts of a few Jewish people, who sent me to Washington. As I walked up to the barracks, fear came over me, and I decided to go to Baltimore, where I remained with a Jewish missionary until the last of April. Then I returned to Washington, went to the commanding officer, Lieutenant-Colonel Langfitt, and told him why I was giving myself up.

He said: "Are you a Jew and a believer in Jesus? Are you willing to give yourself up for his sake? Do you know what it means to give yourself up? It means three or four years in the penitentiary and to be dishonorably discharged."

I told him that I would gladly do anything to make this matter right before man and before God.

"I am also a Jew," he replied, "and I do not know how you can believe in Jesus and suffer these things for his sake."

Then he doubted my being a deserter. I begged him to put me in the guard-house and to go and investigate the matter.

He said, "I wish that I had the power to set you free now; but you are too honorable a man to call the guard to take you to the guard-house, and so I will walk there with you myself."

Upon coming to the guard-house, he called the sergeant of the guard and said, "Sergeant, do not search this boy, for I know that he will not take in anything but that which is lawful."

He then asked me whether I wanted to stay in the big cell with the rest of the prisoners or go into one small cell by myself. I asked him for one by myself so that I might study the Bible.

When he was bidding me good-by, he said: "For the first time I shake a prisoner's hand, and I must say that I do not look upon you as a prisoner but as the most honorable man that we have in this post, and I must confess that you have done a most honorable thing in the sight of man and God, and I will help you with all that lies within my power to make everything easy for you."

The next morning the lieutenant-colonel came into the guard-house asking for me. When I came near the door, he reached out his hand and grasped mine, saying, "Neither my wife nor I have slept during the night, and I have decided to recommend you for a year's clemency, so that you will have only two years to serve."

It did not sound very good to me, but I went into the guard-house and prayed. The thought came to me, "Can you not trust the Lord to carry you through all these difficulties?" I said to myself, "Yes, I leave all in the hands of the Lord."

After a few weeks the court was detailed. The president of the court was Captain Koester, who, I was informed, was an infidel. The next man of his court, Captain Ottwell, was a Christian Scientist, and the rest of the court, including eleven officers, were Roman Catholics. They detailed Lieutenant Rockwell to be my counsel for defense. He came up to the court-house and said:

"You are a Jew, are you not?"

"Yes."

"And you believe in Jesus Christ, do you not?"

"Yes."

"I have no use for Jews, especially for a turncoat, and I will see that you get the limit of the court."

This broke me all up, and I said, "Lieutenant, if you can, God will let you go ahead."

I then walked into my cell and knelt down to pray, broken-hearted. The scripture came to me, "Fear them not; for I the Lord thy God shall fight for you." I rejoiced to know that the Lord was fighting my battles and that he would do it well. Thirteen days afterwards I was tried.

When I came to the court, the lieutenant came to me with a piece of paper in his hand and said: "I am sorry for the words which I spoke to you, but I have suffered for them, and with God's help I will recommend you to clemency. The same Lord that saved you has also saved me."

The judge of the court asked me what I would plead to the charge.

"I plead guilty to the charge of desertion and violation of the forty-seventh article of war."

He asked me again if I knew what it meant to plead guilty. I answered that I knew.

He then asked me what my plea on the specification of the forty-seventh article of war was.

"Guilty," I answered.

He said to the court, "I want to make plain to this boy the solemnity of these charges, that he may know the consequences thereof." He then asked me if I had any pleas to make.

I told him no, and repeated the scripture that the Lord had given me: "Fear them not; for I the Lord thy God shall fight for you." I said, "I fear you not, for my Lord will fight for me and will deliver me."

Then the counsel for the defense arose and made this statement:

"Fellow Officers: You all know what a bitter man I was against the Jews. You know that I was not going to make any plea, but to let this boy get all that the court could give him, and be sorry afterwards that the court could not give him more. But the same God that he serves troubled me and made me sick, as you know, until I realized that the same God must be my God and the same Savior my Savior; and furthermore, the same Jesus that saved this Jewish boy has saved me also."

The court was greatly surprized, but my counsel went on further and handed the court a paper and explained verbally the different reasons for his pleas until tears came to the eyes of Captain Koester, Captain Ottwell, and the different members of the court. Four of the worst officers arose and recommended me for eighteen months' clemency and thirteen dollars a month fine and reinstatement to duty.

The recommendation of the court was sent to the Department Commander of the East, Major-General Leonard A. Woods, who earnestly considered the case, according to his statement, for several hours, not knowing what to do. He also expressed himself by saying that if he had full power to release me, he would gladly do so, without any punishment. Also, through prayer and petitions to the Lord the case reached President Taft, the Adjutant-General of the army, and then it reached Brigadier-General Davis, who was the Judge-Advocate General of the United States Army. They also had notified the Department Commander to be as lenient as he could before the case had reached the War Department in Washington.

In fifteen days after my trial, the sentence came back approved by the Department Commander for eighteen months' clemency and thirteen dollars' fine a month and reinstatement to duty to serve out my enlistment.

While I was in the guard-house in Washington Barracks, District of Columbia, serving the sentence imposed upon me for the charge heretofore mentioned, I was sawing wood one day, when a fellow prisoner hit me with a piece of wood behind my ear and knocked me down. About two months later this prisoner was saved, and the other prisoners became bitter against me, for they believed that I was the cause of the conversion of one of the worst men in the guard-house. I learned later that a number of the officers were converted.

After I left the Washington Barracks, I went to Ft. Slocum, New York. From there I was sent to Ft. Sheridan, where I was assigned to Battery F, Fifth Field Artillery. After I had been there two days, I asked permission of Lieutenant Osborn to hold religious services in front of the battery. On account of its being so cold, he told me to go into the pool-room and hold services if I thought my God was living.

I went into the pool-room, where they were playing pool, and began to preach the gospel. Two balls were thrown at me, and I was also hit across the back with the thick end of a cue. They took me to the hospital and after a short time came back and said that the Jew would not preach Jesus Christ any more. After another week I felt impressed to preach the gospel again. While I was preaching, the cook came out of the kitchen with a pail of hot lard and threw it on me. I was burned on both of my hands and arms.

While I was at the hospital, black poison set in, and the doctor said my arm must be cut off. I told him that I would not submit to any operation; that as I suffered this for the gospel's sake, the Lord would heal my arm. Five weeks later he looked at my arm, as the poison was getting worse in my system, and he said, "If I do not cut off this arm, you are going to die from the effects of blood-poisoning." I said that I still had faith in God that he would heal this arm for his glory.

"What church do you belong to?" he inquired.

"I belong to the church of God," I answered.

"Your arm can not heal," he replied and began to laugh.

Several days afterward the poison had come up to my shoulder. When the doctor saw it, he said, "The only thing to do is to cut your arm off at the shoulder."

I told him that I had more faith than ever in God that he would heal my arm, even after my whole body should be poisoned. I believed that the Lord would heal me for his glory.

That night my fever was 104, and the doctor was called. He gave orders to put me into a bathtub full of ice-water, but after I came out I was much worse, and they said I could not live through the night. At five o'clock the next morning a sudden change came and my arm turned a yellowish color and the discharge ceased little by little. When the doctor came, he said, "I had thought that the arm must be cut off, but now it will get well." In two weeks I was able to use my arm as well as ever and was again assigned to duty.

After coming out of the hospital I preached much more the unsearchable riches of Christ, for which at different times I was cast into prison. The post-commander of Ft. Sheridan told me that I might just as well use the gymnasium-hall to preach the gospel six nights in the week. While I preached there, a number of souls were brought to the Lord.

While I was at Ft. Sheridan, a letter came to me from my mother stating that if I wanted to save her life I should turn back to Judaism and forsake the impostor Jesus, and that if I would do this they would receive me back again with full honor, as I was defiled before them and the only means to save her life was for me to turn back from this heathen belief. I wrote her as follows:

"My Dear Mother: I have received your letter and thank you very much for it. I do really love you, but my love for you now is much different than before. I love you because the Lord Jesus loved you and died for you. Yet if my accepting Jesus will not and can not save you from dying, then my rejecting him will not save you either, and I can not forsake the Lord Jesus."

About two months later I received a cable-message saying that the last words of my mother were, "My only son is the cause of my death." After that period they made a burial service, took all my little belongings, put them in a casket and buried it, and put a stone on the grave, signifying that I died on October 29, 1908. After this they mourned for me for eight days. Now though I am supposed to be dead to my family and to my nation, yet I am glad that I am alive for Christ and still preaching the unsearchable riches of our Lord and Savior Jesus Christ to my own people as well as to the other nations. The Lord has enabled me to preach free of charge to any and every one and to give unto them freely even as I have freely received. This scripture has been very real to me since that time: "All things work together for good to them that love God, to them who are the called according to his purpose."

In 1912 my father died, leaving me of his large estate five dollars to buy a rope and soap to hang myself if I did not come back to Judaism.

The foregoing account of my conversion has been written after nearly seven years of experience and preaching the unsearchable riches of Christ to my own people as well as to Gentile people in this country, in the Islands of the Azores, in Spain, France, Germany, Italy, Syria, Egypt, Palestine, Greece, and Austria.

The most bitter people against the gospel I have found are my own people. The gospel has been misrepresented to them, and they have not been made to realize the heart experience. There are over 12,000,000 Jewish people in this world, yet there are very few faithful and tried missionaries amongst them to explain to them the way of salvation. However, the comparatively little work that has been done amongst them has met with large results despite the bitter persecution. I am deeply encouraged and comforted to see how open and receptive they are, although they bitterly persecute the one who comes in the name of the Lord. Saul of Tarsus was a great persecutor of Christianity, but finally yielded and became a true follower of Jesus Christ.

May God help us as Christians to see our great privilege in giving the Jews the gospel and praying for them that their blindness may depart and that they may see that the Lord Jesus is the only way, the truth, and the light.

Among Mohammedans in Egypt

EXPERIENCE NUMBER 8

Nothing is said in the New Testament about the persons who first related the story of the cross in Egypt. But there is a universal tradition that the Evangelist Mark went to Egypt and preached the gospel with great success until he was martyred for the name of Jesus Christ. His head is believed by the Copts to have been buried in the place where the Coptic Church in Alexandria now stands. From the records of history it is clear that the Christian religion was carried to Egypt a few years after the ascension of our Lord, that many in Egypt accepted the new religion before the close of the first century, and that the numbers rapidly increased until Egypt became Christian and churches filled the land. Abyssinia, too, whether through the Ethiopian's return to his country after his baptism or through others, also accepted the Christian faith, and many of her people retain the Christian name and boldly defend a form of Christian doctrine to this day.

The church in Egypt, as we learn from the pages of history, passed through the fires of persecution as other churches did in the Roman Empire, and many suffered martyrdom for their unwillingness to deny Him who redeemed them with his precious blood. The persecution in Egypt especially was severe in the reign of Diocletian. Milner says on the authority of Eusebius: "Egypt suffered extremely. Whole families were put to various kinds of death; some by fire, others by water, others by decollation, after horrible tortures. Some perished by famine, others by crucifixion, and of these, some in common manner. Others were fastened with their heads downwards and preserved alive that they might die by hunger. Sometimes ten, at other times thirty, sixty, and once a hundred men and women with their children, were murdered in one day by various torments. And there was still the appearance of joy among them. They loved Christ above all, and bravely as well as humbly met death for Christ's sake."

But as the years passed on, great importance was laid on fasting, hermitage, and image-worship, and little by little they lost sight of the merits of Christ's life, sufferings, and death. Today the majority of the Copts are far away from the gospel purity of doctrine and are bound with the chains of superstition, and need help to loosen themselves from such chains that they may enjoy the light and liberty of the gospel.

THE REAL CHARACTER OF ISLAM

The population of Egypt today is 12,000,000, of which 90 per cent are followers of Mohammed. Mohammedanism entered Egypt in 638 A. D., and from that time it has continued to be the prevailing religion. I will now mention briefly the ethics of Mohammedanism in order to give the reader some idea about the pollution, corruption, brutality, and wickedness that exist among the adherents of this false religion.

"Islam," says Adolph Wuttke, "finds its place in the history of the religious and moral spirit, not as a vital organic member, but as violently interrupting the course of this history, and which is to be regarded as an attempt of heathenism to maintain itself erect under an outward monotheistic form against Christianity."

The ethics of Islam bear the character of an outwardly and crudely conceived doctrine of righteousness. Conscientiousness in the sphere of the social relations, faithfulness to conviction and to one's word, and the bringing of an action into relation to God are its bright points; but there is a lack of heart-depth of a basing of the moral in love. The highest good is the outwardly and very sensuously conceived happiness of the individual.

Among Islamites the potency of sin is not recognized; evil is only an individual, not a historical, power; hence there is no need of redemption, but only of personal works on the basis of prophetic instruction. Mohammed is only a teacher, not an atoner. God and man remain strictly external to and separate from each other. God, no less individually conceived of than man, comes into no real communion with man; and as moral, acts not as influenced by such a communion, but only as an isolated individual. The ideal basis of the moral is faith in God and in his Prophet; the moral life, conceived as mainly consisting in external works, is not a fruit of received salvation, but a means for the attainment of the same. Pious works, particularly prayer, fasting, and almsgiving, and pilgrimage to Mecca, work salvation directly of themselves. Man has nothing to receive from God but the Word, and nothing to do for God but good works; of inner sanctification there is no thought. Thus, among Islamites today we find, instead of true humility, only proud work-righteousness. Nothing but the enjoyment of wine, of swine-flesh, of the blood of strangled animals, and games of chance are forbidden.

After this summary of the real character of Mohammedan ethics, an account of its practical teaching and effect will make the picture more vivid to the reader, although still darker.

THE MOSLEM IDEA OF SIN

Moslem doctors define sin as "a conscious act of a responsible being against known law." They divide sin into "great" and "little" sins. Some say there are seven great sins: idolatry, murder, false charges of adultery, wasting the substance of orphans, taking interest on money, desertion from Jihad, and disobedience to parents. Mohammed himself said, "The greatest of sins before God is that you call another like unto the God who created you, or that you murder your child from an idea that he or she will eat your victuals, or that you commit adultery with your neighbor's wife."

All sins except great ones are easily forgiven, as God is merciful and clement. What Allah (God) allows is not sin. What Allah or his Prophet forbids is sin, even should he forbid what seems right to the conscience. It is as great an offense to pray with unwashed hands as to tell a lie, and pious Moslems who nightly break the seventh commandment will shrink from a tin of English meat for fear they will be defiled by eating swine's flesh. Oh, what ignorance! The false prophet Mohammed said: "One cent of usury which a man takes for his money is more grievous than thirty-six fornications, and whosoever has done so is worthy of hell-fire. Allah is merciful in winking at the sins of his favorites (the prophets and those who fight his battles), but is a quick avenger of all infidels and idolaters."

THE LOW IDEAL OF CHARACTER OF ISLAM

A stream can not rise higher than its source. The measure of the moral stature of Mohammed is the source and foundation of all moral ideas of Islam. His conduct is the standard of character. We need not be surprized, therefore, that the ethical standard is so low among his followers. Raymond Lull, the first missionary to Moslems, used to show in his preachings that Mohammed had none of the seven cardinal virtues, and was guilty of the seven deadly sins. He may have gone too far, but it would not be difficult to show that pride, lust, envy, and anger were prominent traits in the Prophet's character.

To take an example, what Mohammed taught regarding truthfulness is convincing. There are two authenticated sayings of his given in the traditions on the subject of lying: "When a servant of God tells a lie, his guardian angels move away to the distance of a mile because of the badness of its smell." "Verily a lie is allowable in three cases—to women, to reconcile friends, and in war." It is no wonder, then, that among the Prophet's followers and imitators "truth-telling is one of the lost arts" and that perjury is too common to be noticed. As I pass in the streets of Cairo, many times I hear the Moslems utter the word, b'ism Allah, "in the name of God," while the speaker knows very well that his words are altogether a lie.

There are certain things which the ethics of Islam allow, of which it is also necessary to write. They exist, not in spite of Islam, but because of Islam, and because of the teachings of its sacred book.

POLYGAMY, DIVORCE, AND SLAVERY

These three evils are so closely intertwined with the Mohammedan religion, its book, and its prophet, that they can never be wholly abandoned without doing violence to the teaching of the Koran and the example of Mohammed.

A Moslem who lives up to his privileges and follows the example of their saints can have four wives and any number of slave concubines; can divorce at his pleasure; can remarry his divorced wives by a special, though abominable, arrangement; and in addition to all this, if he belong to the Shiah sect he can contract marriages for fun (metaa), which are temporary. The Koran permits a Moslem to marry four legal wives, and to have as many concubines, or slave-girls, as he can support. In Turkey, Moslems call a woman cow.

In Islam, marriage is a kind of slavery; for the wife becomes the slave (rakeek) of her husband, and it is her duty absolutely to obey him in everything he requires of her, except in what is contrary to the laws of Islam. Wife-beating is allowed by the Koran.

The other ethic, which is much worse than all the rest, is slave-trade. According to the Koran, slavery and the slave-trade are divine institutions. From the Koran we learn that all male and female slaves, either married or single, taken as plunder in war are the lawful property of the master, his chattel. Slave-traffic is not only allowed but legislated for by Mohammedan law and made sacred by the example of the Prophet.

For five hundred years Islam has been supreme in Turkey, the fairest and richest portion of the Old World, and what is the result today? The treasury is bankrupt; progress is blocked; "instead of wealth, universal poverty; instead of comeliness, rags; instead of commerce, beggary."

Such are the chief tenets and religious requirements of Mohammedans in Egypt, Turkey, and in other countries where the people believe in the Koran. Christianity exists in Turkey by a kind of sufferance. The Turks hate, ridicule, foster pride and passion toward Christians; the ignorant populace are taught by their learned men to regard themselves infinitely better than any Christian. The mosques are generally the hotbeds of fanaticism. The usual manner of speaking of the Christian was and still is to call him, in Turkey, "Imansig Kevour" (unbeliever); in Egypt, "Nasrani," (Nazarene), or "Ya din el kalb," (you dog). Peace, harmony, and happiness in the homes of Mohammedans are of a very transitory nature.

Mohammedans may be stedfast and unswerving in their faith and yet guilty of some of the most heinous crimes. Having lived among them, I have had many opportunities to learn of their treachery as well as of their sterling qualities. The Mohammedans are in great need of the gospel of Jesus Christ, which is a gospel of pardon, peace, purity, righteousness, and true wisdom.

Notwithstanding the fact that from their earliest childhood their ideas are perverted by their traditions and false teaching, and their consciences defiled through their vain religion, the melting power of the Spirit of God reaches some of their hearts when the gospel of Jesus Christ is preached. Their lives of deception bring to them many a snare, yet from among their ranks in the Orient have come some of the most staunch ministers of the gospel. Gross darkness once reigned throughout the land of Egypt, and now fervent prayers are ascending to the throne of God for the light of the gospel to drive the spiritual darkness from the hearts of the people.

A Daughter's Faith Rewarded

EXPERIENCE NUMBER 9

I was brought up by Christian parents, that is, they were strict church-going people; but I never knew what it was to have a change of heart, though I feared God and did at times try to draw near to him.

It was after I graduated from school that I met those who believe in living holy lives. I was very much impressed with them, but I did not give my heart to God at that time. I continued to meet them and after some months became convicted that I was a sinner and under the wrath of God. Having attended church and Sunday-school from childhood, I had considered myself a Christian; but when the Bible standard was lifted up before me, I soon saw my true condition.

One day while alone I yielded myself fully to God, and he received me into his family. I did not know at that time, though I was very happy in my new-found love, what a treasure I had really found; but the eighteen years I have

already spent in His service verifies to me that the path of
the righteous shineth more and more unto the perfect day.

A spirit of love and gratitude begets a spirit of service. I
wanted to do something for God, so began visiting the sick.
Soon I felt a desire to go into the work of the Lord, but this
step was much opposed in my home, my family having had
a life of worldly honor mapped out for me. I waited, hoping
a way would open for me to go, but it seemed my friends
were becoming more opposed to the life I had chosen. I
was forced to leave home against the wishes of my friends,
especially my dear mother, but I see more clearly now than
I did then that God's hand was in it and that he was leading
me.

Mother was so displeased that she took steps to disinherit
me, but afterwards, through the persuasion of others, she
relented. She also forbade me the privilege of returning
home, but in this she also relented. I wondered at this
change in my dear mother, who was one of the best of
mothers, for this new life I had received seemed to have
made a great gulf between us. It certainly had made a
marked change in the once rebellious, self-willed girl, and I
could not understand why my mother, who had spent many
anxious moments because of my wilfulness, was not
rejoicing instead of opposing me. I now see that my course
thwarted her worldly ambitions for me; hence the
bitterness.

I had spent a number of years working for the Master,
which were very profitable and beneficial to my soul. To
me it was like God's training-college. My mother came to
visit me sometimes, vainly hoping I would return with her.
She told me that if I would just return home she would buy
me worldly vanities, such as fine dresses, etc., which I had

once loved. She could not understand when I told her I did not want them any more. She even told me I could receive the attentions of a certain young man who for her sake I had once refused. But that fancy also had been removed far from me, and I praised God as I explained to her what a change had been wrought in me.

About one year after this my mother had a severe nervous attack. She came to where I was living, saying that she wanted to make her peace with God and die. Some ministers and I had prayer with her, and God graciously pardoned her soul. Oh the joy that filled my heart when I saw my dear mother humble herself before the Lord! She not only received pardon, but received a divine touch in her body also. She became a bold witness before all our friends and relatives to what God had done for her. It seemed she could never praise him enough. Though she was a woman of very strong character and personality, she became as gentle and teachable as a little child. Her nature seemed to be entirely changed. While I write this, tears of gratitude flow because of the greatness of God's salvation. She spent a few happy months here below, and then God took her.

Missionary Experiences in British West Indies

EXPERIENCE NUMBER 10

It was a warm, sultry morning late in December. The tropical air was scarcely fanned by a breeze. The missionary heard the peculiar tapping of the postman at the gate and hurried to get his morning mail. He took the single letter that was handed him, and with a pleasant nod to the postman broke the seal as he stepped back to the veranda.

It was a long letter; so before reading it the man sank into a chair and glanced away to the gleaming sea; but meeting only the dazzling light there, he let his eyes rest upon the distant blue-green mountains for a moment. Then for some time he was occupied with the contents of this lengthy letter. It was written in a neat, scholarly manner, and the missionary noted it all as he read.

As he finished reading, a bright-faced woman came through the garden with a baby in her arms. "Come here, Jennie," he said; and his wife came quickly to him. "Here is a letter, Jennie, that requires very careful answering. You know how busy I am; so I will commit this into your care. This person, a Mr. K. L. Jones, has asked many questions on the church and other points of doctrine." He looked up as he spoke, and, finding the baby holding out its chubby arms to him, he took it and handed the letter to his wife.

Thoughtfully she took it and began reading. She loved to write letters, and this, she felt, was her special part of the work. But here she perceived she had a task that was very difficult; for the writer, evidently a scholar, had put forth a dozen numbered questions that must be carefully answered or this dear soul would be hindered from walking in the truth. God would give the needed wisdom, she knew, and she folded the letter back into its envelope and sat meditating on the different points he had raised. After a while, she asked:

"How was the meeting last night?"

"Very good! Brother Owen spoke, and he did very well indeed. He used the text: 'Herein is my Father glorified, that ye bear much fruit; so shall ye be my disciples.' Several came forward for help afterwards. Ah, by the way, do you remember Sister Tilton? She was out to meeting last night."

"Sister Tilton? She must be a new sister!"

"Ah, well, perhaps we did not tell you about her. This young girl came to meeting once some time ago, but afterwards became very ill. Her folks wanted the doctor for her, but she refused, not telling them why. But as her sickness increased, they became alarmed and insisted on calling the doctor. But the girl still refused the medicine. The doctor said she would probably not live. Her people begged to know the reason for her refusal to take the medicine, and she then said that she had been to the church of God meeting and had been made very happy, and that she believed if they would send for the elders of that church she should be healed. So word came, and Brother Owen went and anointed her in accordance with Jas. 5:14, 15. She has been getting better right along, and tonight she was at the meeting. She is saved now and seems to have a clear experience."

"Thank God!" was the hearty response. "How I should have loved to be at the meeting last night!—but for the present here is my meeting, and here is my work," and, catching up the baby and waving the letter happily, she ran into the house at the sound of children's voices within.

After the baby had been bathed and put to sleep, and the other children were sitting quietly at play on the side veranda, Sister Patience settled herself with her Bible at her

husband's desk to answer this important letter. Bowing her
head she besought God for this soul and for wisdom to
answer his difficult questions aright. Then taking up her
pen, she began the letter. She was so glad to write; she
loved writing; and the joy of it always seemed to get into
the very letters and shine back from the pages. She
addressed Mr. Jones cordially and kindly, and then took up
the substance of the letter itself. In calling his attention to
certain truths she referred to the Bible time after time, and
again and again she prayed, for the letter seemed
particularly important to her. Long she meditated over
some of the knotty questions, endeavoring to find the
wisest explanation. Sometimes she was interrupted by the
children just when she most needed to be quiet; but she had
learned that interruptions often come as blessings in
disguise, for often God had given thoughts that were
clearer and better when she had patiently gone to attend to
the children, and when she was free to return to her work
she had found an answer preparing itself in her mind
without an effort on her part. Thus, after several hours of
close application, she finished the letter and sent it off with
a trusting spirit.

Sister Patience hoped to receive an answer to her letter
immediately, but week after week passed, and there was no
response. Dread began to creep upon her that this soul
would not accept the truth. She took him earnestly to God
many times and trusted that God would in some way
overrule. However, as four months passed and she had not
heard again, she gave him over as being no longer
interested.

Then it was that one morning there came, to her surprize, a
letter in the same fine handwriting. How cordially he
wrote! He thanked her for answering the former letter so

fully and said he had been searching and proving her answers by the Word during the long interval. And now there were still a few points remaining that he disagreed with her upon; again she found a few numbered questions to answer.

These, like the first, were very shrewd, puzzling questions, and only sagacious answers would satisfy the inquirer. Again Sister Patience labored over the letter with prayer and meditation. Then, leaning hard upon God, she wrote another encouraging letter setting forth expositions of Scripture as clearly as possible. This time she invited her correspondent to a series of meetings they were expecting to hold during the coming winter season, when they hoped to have with them one or two ministers from America for a short period.

Again she waited long for an answer; but this time she did not give him up. Several months passed, and then one of the brethren, a colporteur, came. He had been away for several months, and Sister Patience was very glad to see him.

"And tell me now, Brother Delworth," she said, after the first greetings were over, "where have you been all this time?"

"Mostly in Arendon and Lawney. I went from Panville to Mayfield, and from there to Paldings."

"Paldings! You were at Paldings? Do you know one K. L. Jones?" asked Sister Patience with great interest.

"Ah yes, a fine old gentleman, a school-teacher. He is saved. I sold him some books. He seems very much interested. And, by the way, he asked me to say to you when I should see you that he hoped to come over to the meeting next month, when the brethren are here from America. You will hear from him soon."

The time was drawing near for the coming of the brethren from America. Arrangements had been made for a meeting during their stay, which would be only for a few days. And then one day a letter came from Brother Jones inquiring as to the date of the meeting, and saying that if possible he should like to attend it. So again Sister Patience wrote him, urging him to be at the meeting, if possible.

Thus it was that during the exciting days of the meeting, when many from different parts of the country had gathered in to meet the brethren from America in this meeting, Sister Patience first met Brother Jones. It happened in this way: One morning before meeting-time, she was passing through the little sitting-room in her home, when she noticed a fine-looking native man of venerable appearance sitting at one side of the room. People were all about him, but he was looking over some tracts that had been handed him. Making her way to him, she said:

"Good morning, Brother, I have not met you before, have I?"

"Ah, no," he said, and, quickly rising, he gave her a courteous bow. "Can this be Sister Patience? My name is K. L. Jones, of Paldings."

"How glad I am to meet you!" she replied. And then followed an animated conversation in which she was able to recognize and admire the fine qualities of his matured mind. Finally he expressed the desire to speak with the foreign brethren himself, and so an audience was arranged for him after the next service. Then it was, Sister Patience learned afterwards, that Brother Jones inquired deeply into the subjects of sanctification and baptism. Later in the day it was announced that there would be a baptismal service early the next morning to accommodate Brother Jones, who was to return home by an early train.

Some years have passed since then. God has wonderfully used the dear old brother, and a congregation has been raised up about him, who look up to him as their pastor. These are backward mountain people where he has labored, yet such has been his patience and faithfulness and love that they have become established in holiness and truth. Brother Jones, as we call him, is becoming feeble now, but he is still standing faithful as the shepherd of this little flock, faithful unto death.

Does it pay to use patience and prayer when dealing with precious souls? Ah yes; eternity alone can tell all that it means.

The Rescue of an Australian Lad

EXPERIENCE NUMBER 11

It was in the town of Goulbourne, New South Wales, Australia, that I began my career in life. Until I reached the age of four years, a prosperous father provided the comforts of a good home, but a great change took place upon my suddenly being left fatherless. A few months later found me in a little town on the St. Lawrence River, in the Providence of Ontario, Canada. I had accompanied my mother to this place, but she soon placed me with a strange family and went to a distant city.

As I was now separated from every family tie, life began in real earnest. It was also the beginning of a record of many interesting and often sad experiences extending over a number of years. In my wanderings in different parts of Canada and in many localities of the United States, the incidents varied all the way from being rescued from drowning to landing in jail as a vagrant. Space forbids a detailed account of my experience, which to me affords material for interesting and often regretful recollection. It may, however, all be summed up and described as analogous with the casting of an innocent infant into the mighty Niagara River to be swept along at the mercy of the on-rushing and maddening current, which knows no relenting, but bears its victim to an untimely end over the brink of the mighty falls. There destruction on the ragged rocks below awaits it unless an unseen hand should miraculously dip into the water and save that form for life and service.

Thank God, in his tender mercy he stretched forth his hand to rescue my poor, lost, helpless soul from the turbulent rapids of sin when I was seventeen years of age. He set me on the solid rock of his truth and gave me the Holy Spirit as an eternal guide and propelling power. He has proved to be a comforter in whom I can safely put my trust when stemming the rising tide of unbelief and doubt.

It is with thanksgiving that I can at the present time recount the divine care of which I have been the object, so far in my pilgrimage through life. I rejoice to be a partaker of the Father's love, which is pure, warm, and changeless. There is an abiding assurance of safety so long as I walk in the path of obedience to his will and trust implicitly in his mighty power to keep my feet while I take steps toward the threshold of heaven. I am grateful, also, for a soul-conviction that the most worthy, most desirable and glorious life is the one that finds its outlet in the glad service of love to God and discovers complete happiness in serving others. A soul without Christ is like an idle straw driven at the mercy of the wind, but the soul redeemed through the blood of Jesus will experience a sweet essence that turns the unfruitful life into a garden of unspeakable delights.

Heathen Customs in China

EXPERIENCE NUMBER 12

To those who have been reared in Christian nations, it is difficult to conceive of the vague ideas of the true worship of the Creator, that are really bred and born into the worshipers of idols. Generation upon generation, for thousands of years, have been taught the same form of worship, or nearly so, until such heathen ideas and doctrines have become just as much a part of their nature as is any other sinful disposition.

Having been a personal observer of a few of their customs, I shall here be mentioning what I have seen, with a prayer that my account may at least help the reader more fully to appreciate the access that every worshiper of the true God has to the bountiful storehouse of blessings provided by our Creator.

For nearly five years I lived a short distance outside a large city in China. Almost as far as we could see in any direction, the hills and valleys were dotted with little mounds. (Some of the valleys, however, were under cultivation.) How came all these little mounds, some round, some long, some large and some small, some carefully covered over with fresh green sod, and others greatly weather-beaten and nearly washed away by the rains of the season? These mysterious little mounds mark the last resting-places of thousands of Chinese. Should the mortal remains in a mound be those of a child, little or no attention is shown it; but should it be those of a father or a mother, the relatives who are left behind do not fail to show great respect and attention to the spirit of the departed one. Should they not render such attention, they believe the spirit has power to inflict upon them great sorrow and adversity.

Some of their methods of showing respect I have observed to be as follows: After a body is prepared for burial, candles and incense are kept burning, near the head and the feet; also bowls of rice and other food, with a pair of chopsticks, are placed within easy reach, for the use of the spirit. On the day of the funeral some one is hired to scatter representations of paper money along the road, just ahead of the bier. In determining the position of the coffin at the grave, great care is taken to have the head turned directly toward some favorite temple, that the spirit may have no trouble in finding its way there. Before the casket is covered with sod, a religious ceremony is held in this way: All the relatives present, beginning with the nearest kinsman, kneel down and bow from one to three times, to the one whom they now hold in such great esteem. Even the tiniest children are taught to thus bow before and reverence their ancestor. This being finished, there is then kindled, at the foot of the casket, a small fire of paper money, by which means they believe the value thereof is transported to the spirit-world for the use of their departed one.

A day or two after the funeral, and on special feast-days, the near relatives carry food to the grave and offer the food to the spirit by placing it in bowls before the grave. They also again burn paper money or incense. While the fire burns, and the food remains to be received by the spirit, a woman, usually the nearest relative, kneels by the side of the grave and begins a long-drawn-out season of lamenting and wailing for the sorrow that has come upon her on account of the death of the one by whose grave she is kneeling. She soon almost prostrates herself. During this season of weeping, she enumerates over and over, all the virtues and good qualities of the departed one, and begs him to come back to her. She usually continues in this frenzy until some one who has accompanied her, pulls her up, bidding her cease the wailing. The bowls of food previously offered to the spirit are now given to the children or carried home for others to eat. By this manner of worship the woman is supposed to show great honor and reverence to the deceased, whether he was her father, brother, husband, or son.

Well do I remember the strange feelings that came over me the first few times I witnessed from my window such a scene as I have just described. I felt such a longing to go to the weeping woman, put my arms around her, and comfort her sad heart. But to my utter astonishment, within two or three minutes after all her touching lamentations she was up laughing, talking, and having a jovial time with those about her! Whence came those agonizing groans, and whither had they flown? Had "He who is touched with the feeling of our infirmities" comforted her heart? Had the God of heaven, who is a present help in every time of trouble, stretched forth his loving hand to dry her tears of sorrow? Ah, no; sadly enough, no. Believe me, reader, when I say that these superstitious women worshiping the spirits of departed ones have a form of sorrow and make a great pretense of distress, but that, in reality, it is only a custom or habit which has been copied from their grandmothers for generations back. This may seem hard to believe, but one thing which convinced me the quickest was that they all have precisely the same tune or swing to their wailing. After hearing it once or twice, you always recognize it afterwards, wherever you are, whether you see the person or not. It is like a recitation or song committed to memory. There may be no signs whatsoever of sorrow until after the woman has taken her place beside the grave, when she immediately begins in tones that could probably be heard, on a quiet day, a quarter of a mile away, and continues wailing in the same pitch until some one bids her cease, when her outward appearance of sorrow ceases as abruptly as it began. I do not mean to say that never is there any real sorrow mingled with the outward form. There may be, but it is the outward form which constitutes the worship and which every woman seems to know how to perform when the occasion presents itself.

Now permit me to tell something concerning the worship of idols. Originally, I had the idea that the inside arrangement of a heathen temple was very much the same as that of a Christian chapel; namely, that seats were orderly arranged for the worshipers and that the idols would be standing in the front where the pulpit should be. But upon my first visit to a temple, I saw that I was mistaken. At or near the temple door stand two very large, fierce-looking idols, known as guards of the temple. Arranged all around the sides are numerous other idols, of various kinds and sizes. But in the center of the building stands one or more large idols, who are supposed to impart different kinds of blessings to the worshiper. Standing near by are a number of incense-pots, from which ascends smoke continuously on worship-days. On the floor can be seen a number of thick, round mats, on which the worshipers kneel as they bow before the idols. They do not have fixed hours of worship and all assemble at the appointed time, but at any time throughout the day few or many may go in and bow before whatever idols are supposed to bestow the kinds of blessings desired. The idol is not supposed to give out the blessing at the time the worshiper bows before him, as some readers may have believed. For instance, at the beginning of a new year, if a man bows before the god of wealth, he does not expect the idol to hand out money to him, but rather he expects that during the coming year he shall have financial prosperity.

I remember once seeing a father bow before an idol, then take his three little children, one by one, show them how to kneel upon the mat, fold their little hands, and bump their heads several times upon the floor in front of the hideous idol, of which the little ones were afraid. The father noticed that I was observing closely the procedure. When it was all finished, he looked at me with a smile, as if to say, "Didn't they do well?"

These things can not but make sad the heart of a child of God. Catching a glimpse now and again of a bit of real idol-worship helps one to realize that the church, in evangelizing the world, has indeed a mighty undertaking.

From a human standpoint, it may seem impossible, but with God all things are possible.

Deliverance from Discouragements and Extremism

EXPERIENCE NUMBER 13

Along the narrow way that leads to heaven, the Christian meets with many experiences that to him seem strange and inexplicable. That at times he should walk in light and then again in darkness; that sometimes he should run with ease and then again be compelled (as Bunyan puts it) "to fall from running to going, and from going to clambering upon his hands and his knees, because of the steepness of the place"; that he should stand today upon the mountain-top of glory and tomorrow find himself plunged into the valley of despondency and gloom; that today he should feel so clearly his Savior's presence, and tomorrow be left seemingly so entirely to himself; all these and many other things of like nature tend to puzzle and confuse the souls of pilgrims on the way to glory. That discouragements and disappointments would come from outside sources almost all have expected, but that the inward life should be changeful and varied in any wise many have not thought consistent with true Christian experience.

VARIED EXPERIENCES

Some, upon discovering that the Christian's pathway leads
not always through verdant valleys and beside still waters,
conclude that the way is too often rough and that therefore
the prize is not worth the running, become discouraged and
turn back into sin. Others, after wondering and seeking in
vain for a way always bright and easy, and learning that all
Christians have similar experiences of inward light and
shade, conclude that these things are part of the way and
determine to take them as a matter of course and make the
best of them. They consider the prize too great to miss, and
so they press on at any cost, having settled down to endure
what must be endured and to enjoy what may be enjoyed,
hoping some day for an end to it all, but never discovering
the causes, or being able to think the thoughts of God
concerning their difficulties.

Another class can not be satisfied with this condition of
mingled light and shade. Their souls must ever see the face
of God, and with nothing short of that can they abide
content. They would make any sacrifice if only the glory
and joy they desire might be theirs, and without it they can
not be still. Everywhere they turn crying, "Wherefore
hidest thou thy face," "Make me to know my transgression
and my sin" (Job 13:23, 24); and, like Job again, 'they go
forward, but he is not there; and backward, but they can not
perceive him'; on the right and left they seek, but can not
find him (Job 23:8, 9). But they never quiet their souls
sufficiently for God to tell them the causes of the
conditions which they so much deplore.

Yet another class of Christians go through like experiences
with the others, but somehow God by his grace enables

their hearts, perhaps after years of struggling, to settle down at last into a state of stillness and calm submission where he can teach them the causes of their troubles and so bring them out into that "wealthy place" which is the normal state of a mature Christian. Then they can sing with Job, "I have heard of thee by the hearing of the ear; but NOW mine eye seeth thee" (Job. 42:5).

In religious as truly as in physical and temporal affairs, there is never an effect without an adequate cause. If the Word of God loses its richness, if darkness falls upon the soul, if it is hard to pray, if there is a lack of victory in any respect, there is a reason, a sufficient cause for such a condition. Let it be understood here that the causes are not always, in fact often are not, sins. Much confusion has arisen from imagining that every chastening of the Lord is the punishment of some sin, when, in fact, each of God's sons must endure chastisement that they may become in a fuller sense partakers of his holiness. Thus, we conclude that all the unpleasant experiences with which we meet in the upward way must be for the sake of eliminating something of self and of conforming us more to the divine image. We do not meet them simply because they are in the way, but they are in the way because we need them. Hence the best way to meet all such things is to bring them quickly to Father, not inquiring impatiently, "Why must I suffer so?" but rather: "What is there in my nature that makes this suffering necessary? What is it that thou art endeavoring to do for me? And how may I conduct myself so as to receive the benefit?"

TESTS IN EARLY CHRISTIAN LIFE

Happy is the child of God who can say that from the day of his conversion he has never sinned nor grieved the Spirit of God. Such, however, has not been the experience of the writer. For several years I was plunged, sometimes within the space of a few hours, from extreme happiness and joy into deepest gloom and sadness. Weeks of walking in the joy of the Lord often terminated in some sad failure, causing untold misery of soul. When faith again gained the victory, praises in the day and songs in the night were mine until some other episode or depression of feeling caused me anxiety and fear. In spite of God's matchless grace and patient endeavor to teach me the lessons of absolute dependence and humble trust in him, this condition continued until gradually and almost imperceptibly my soul reached a place where I seemed past feeling, joy was no longer mine, love seemed a sensation foreign to my heart, the power of prayer was gone, and I felt that God had indeed forsaken me. My testimonies (for I was not conscious of any sin and could not give up my hope in Christ) sounded to my own ears as "tinkling cymbal and sounding brass."

That a soul who commits no known sin and who never loses the determination to serve God could get into such a state seems incredible. Such, however, was my condition, and I have met some who are on the way to just such a place of confusion, others who have reached and are now suffering in the same state of misery, and still others who have passed through and found that sweet rest of soul so plainly promised to all who come to Jesus. Such, then, as may be passing through or who are entering upon such experiences, I trust to be able to show how my feet came to sink into the miry clay and how at last God graciously set

me upon the solid rock of his eternal truth and gave me
new songs of praise and love once again.

A DEEPER SPIRITUAL EXPERIENCE

For the two years intervening between my conversion and
the time when I was enabled to make a complete
consecration and receive an experience which I had not
before attained, I enjoyed and endured the experiences
common to the Christian in his early religious life. Many
times I presented myself to God for cleansing, but as often
failed to receive the Holy Ghost, because I could not
believe unless I should have such manifestations of his
incoming as some others had received. At last, in
desperation, being confident that I had yielded all to God, I
determined to believe that he did cleanse my heart and give
me the Holy Spirit whether I ever received any feelings or
not; for had not the immutable God promised, and could his
word be broken? After a severe testing of this decision, the
Holy Spirit came into my heart, cleansing it and filling me
with joy unspeakable and full of glory. "Now," I thought,
"surely all my difficulties are past, and I shall walk in glory
the rest of my life." This bubble soon burst, however; for in
my very testimony to the gracious infilling of the Spirit, I
was shown a degree of self and a lack of humility, which,
had I understood the truth of the matter, should have sent
me in faith to the throne of grace for a supply of what I
lacked, but which, instead, I allowed to throw me into a
state of doubt and fear from which I did not emerge for
some days. The agony of soul which I suffered through not
understanding the fact that I had an individual self-life with
which I must reckon, even though I was sanctified, can be
understood only by those who have become victims to
doubts in a like manner. After a time faith became stronger,

the seasons of depression became fewer, and my soul lived upon the wing. Prayer was a delight; the reading of the Word filled me with praise; meeting the people of God was the joy of my life; and every newly revealed truth made my soul leap for gladness.

GLORYING IN SELF

I came at last to revel in my experiences. Insensibly to myself, I gloried in MY joy, MY victory, MY trueness to God. Others told of trials and difficulties; my testimonies were full of victory and praise, and I rejoiced in the fact. Little by little I began to notice the faults and failures of others, and having begun to think so much of what I was, I had but a little step to go to make a comparison of their faults with my virtues. As I remember, I did this all quite unconsciously; but a brother at last said to me, "I fear you are losing that burning love for others which you once had." Thus reproved, I sought the Father in a very simple prayer that he would fill me again with that sweetness and tenderness so necessary for a child of God. That he answered no one could doubt, least of all I myself. A passion for souls took hold upon me. No labor was too hard, no sacrifice too great, if only I could influence a soul for Jesus. I felt a tenderness of soul toward those whom I had formerly criticized, and whereas I had avoided them, now I felt a drawing toward them, and though I believed (because some in whom I had confidence warned me of it) that they possessed very serious faults, someway I could not see them so plainly.

I was young in years, and oh, so ignorant! If only at that time my wisdom had been equal to my love for God and souls, how much of sorrow I might have been saved! How hard the Spirit of God tried to keep me from taking counsel with self and others! but I had yet to develop that individuality which can stand alone with God in sunshine or tempest and at the same time hold an attitude of humble, submissive love to the brethren. I needed that single eye which sees only God and is not occupied with self or others, except in humbly loving and serving them. Partly through a lack of understanding, but more especially because spiritual pride was gaining a foothold in my heart, making it impossible for me clearly to distinguish the voice of the Spirit of God, I failed to heed his warnings, and entered an experience of darkness and gloom, lighted by a very few rays of his divine presence, which continued over a period of several years.

CRITICIZING OTHERS

Gradually my former experience was repeated. Criticism of others slowly but surely took the place of fervent charity. Contemplation of self and self-complacency supplanted meditation on God and the humble realization of my need of his constant help. Self-sufficiency succeeded humble dependence upon the Lord. All this was utterly uncomprehended by my heart, and soon I began vaguely to wonder why I did not love secret prayer as formerly, why the Word did not seem so good to me as before, and why my thoughts ran so much upon myself and others, whereas in times past the Lord had been the Alpha and Omega of my meditations. My zeal for the truth did not abate. My public devotions were earnest and apparently spiritual, but deep within my soul I knew that there was a difference. However, I was so much taken up with helping others do right that I had not much time to attend to my own needs. God had given me much light, many things for my personal benefit. These I was very anxious for others to see; for if they were good for me, why not for others also? Thus, I endeavored to force my convictions upon all I met. I loved their souls and my actions were born of a desire for their best good, but my attitude must have repelled rather than have attracted them. Anxiety to see every one get as much as possible as quickly as possible, made me oversolicitous and exacting.

At this time I came in contact with some who were inclined to lower the standard in some respects and give more room for looseness of walk and conversation than was expedient. These I looked upon at first with pity, then with indignation, and at last as wilful deceivers. At this stage, I think, the last vestige of divine tenderness vanished from my soul, and I entered the conflict determined to vindicate the truth and see the standard upheld. When efforts were made to discover to me my faults, I could see only theirs. If it was suggested to me that I was lacking in love, I felt that judgments instead of love should be meted out to them. Instead of feeling free in their presence, I felt like avoiding them and almost feared to be with them. This I ascribed to the bad spirit which I felt actuated them. Had I only known how, I might have held to the true standard in righteousness and also in mercy, but I could see no middle ground. Either I was right and they wrong or the opposite was true. And I thought that if I was wrong at all I must be wholly wrong. I had not at that time seen the truth that God judges us by our motives, and condemns or excuses us as we have or do not have an earnest determination to serve him and do his will. So any attempt to recognize those who were failing in doing some of what I was sure was the will of God only resulted in terrible confusion to my soul.

WARNED BY A DREAM

At last God in mercy gave a dream to a brother who was trying to help us. I can not recall it perfectly, but to the best of my recollection, it was somewhat as follows: He thought that he was in the center of a beautiful stream of water, clear as crystal. The banks on each side were perpendicular and very high. On each bank was a large bundle to which was attached a strap. The brother was trying hard, but without success, to pull those bundles into the stream. In the midst of his exertions he awoke. Wondering what was in the bundles, he looked to the Lord and received this solution: The crystal stream represented God's eternal truth; the obstinate bundles contained a list of things which he gave to us somewhat as follows:

TRUTH

Human Reasoning Legality

Zeal for spirituality Great claims to spirituality

Voluntary humility Harshness

Independence Self-sufficiency

Headiness Self-will

Criticism Criticism

Loose handling of Word Zeal for written commands

Exaltation of Spirit above Word Exaction

Undue liberty Bondage

Compromise Fanaticism

INDIFFERENCE OR DOUBTS

Such a revelation of my heart should have helped me, but
so blind was I that the only change it wrought was to turn
the weapons of harshness, criticism, and exaction upon
myself. And for three long miserable years, with a heart
like a stone so far as feelings were concerned, I wrestled
with doubts and fears and tried, oh, so hard! to reach the
standard of spirituality which I had formerly held up for
others. Labor in prayer as I would, the light would not
dispel the darkness, the stony heart would not soften,
except for a short season. Then, how I gloried in the light
and how I mourned when it was dark again! Worse than all
else, there fell upon my soul a state of seeming indifference
to my condition and carelessness toward both God, the
souls of others, and myself. Stir myself out of it, I could
not. Sorrow and joy alike seemed strangers to me. As there
was no blessing, so there was no grief. There was a great
calm, but it was the calm of the grave; it was not peace.
When reproved for causing trials to others, as I often
needed to be, I endeavored not to be guilty of the same
offense again; but no matter what I did, I seemed to
experience no great depth of sorrow. Withal there
developed a lightness quite foreign to what I had been by
nature or grace. I seemed to live only upon the surface, and
to have no ability to reach any depth of grace. This I
deplored, and longed for the blessing of genuine sorrow.
How often I wished that I had never heard the truth if only I
might have the chance to begin all over again!

I lived in circles, making no progress. Daily I prayed for a
return of the joy, love, peace, and victory I had once

known. Sometimes the clouds rifted a little, and I gloried in it, thinking that surely the Lord had heard, and I should be delivered; but soon I would feel the same dulness settle down, leaving in me the same aching void as before. Again and again I tried to repent, thinking that I surely must be a sinner; but I could not work up any earnestness, nor could I find anything in particular of which to repent, only the darkness and general dissatisfaction which I was experiencing. If only I could have begun again; but there seemed no place from which to start, no foundation for my feet, and I felt myself almost entirely swallowed in the quicksand of despondency and discouragement. I realized then the force of the Psalmist's words, "If the foundations be removed, what shall the righteous do?"

DISCOURAGEMENTS

At last my thoughtlessness brought upon me some very severe reproofs. I knew that I was not feeling the weight of them as I should, and I knew also that unless I should be able in some way to see why I did such things I could never get any help. Why should I, who longed to be a soul-winner, be a source of trial to others? Having at last gotten it settled that there was something fundamentally wrong, I determined not to content myself until I should discover what it was. Instead of praying as I had done for so long, for love, joy, etc., I endeavored to humble myself before God and entreat him to show me what was wrong within. I made very slow progress. A day of fasting and prayer revealed nothing. But I would not cease searching my heart. It was very dry praying, for I had no ability even to feel sorry that my condition was so bad; but I had one promise to which I clung desperately: "They that seek the Lord shall not want any good thing" (Psa. 34:10). I could not make myself feel, nor change my state, but I could seek. And it was within my power, as it is within the power of all, to believe that he would be found of me.

At last, little by little, it dawned upon me that I was selfish. The reader may smile, as I myself do now, that I did not know it before. But up to that time I had never stopped to consider why I did things. If I spoke harshly, I was sorry and begged pardon, but it never occurred to me to think why I had spoken so, except that something had not pleased me. If I prayed when I felt inclined and neglected prayer when I did not feel inclined to pray, I knew that I had neglected duty, but to consider why I had neglected it never entered my mind. If words not unto edification escaped my lips, I was ashamed, but my motive for so speaking was unknown to me. But now the Lord showed me clearly that a desire for personal pleasure and profit lurked deep at the root of all those acts of indifference and carelessness. Grateful for one ray of light, I sought again his presence and cried, "But why, O Lord, should I, who have tasted thy divine grace, who have felt the sanctifying power of thy Holy Spirit—why should I be selfish?" My spiritual eye was regaining its sight now and my ear its keenness, so that through many days, in the testimonies of others, through reading, and in prayer and meditation, the answer came by degrees, until at last I understood.

SELF-LOVE AND PURE LOVE

There is, I learned, in every human heart an element called self-love. This is not sinful in itself, being synonymous with that desire for happiness which is the medium through which God appeals to the soul. It is not annihilated in the

sanctified soul, else Jesus could not have said, "Love thy
neighbor as thyself," but it is there subordinated to that
pure love which places God first in all circumstances. To
love the Lord with all the heart, might, mind, and strength
is to love with pure love; but the heart that loves thus still
contains self-love, and it is through this property of the soul
that the sanctified can be tempted. Adam was a perfect
man, with a perfectly pure heart; but when tempted to
obtain something which promised to improve his state and
increase his happiness, he proved that he loved himself by
yielding to the temptation. It is this part of ourselves which
must daily be denied lest it degenerate into selfishness and
cause us trouble. There is a degree to which this self-love
and pure love may become mixed in our service to God.
This had happened in my case.

Pure love serves without any hope of reward. When light
and peace and joy fill the soul, or when grief, sorrow, or
loneliness presses the heart, pure love goes on loving and
serving. Pure love desires, not to be pleased, but to please.
It gives all and demands nothing in return. It loves God, not
so much for what he has done for the soul, or for what the
soul expects him to do for it, but for what he IS. It seeks
him, not so much that it may be blessed, as that it may be a
pleasure to him. It desires, not so much satisfaction for its
own heart, as that he may be satisfied with it. It seeks not
place nor position nor anything, but only that HE may find
pleasure in it, that HE may be able to rejoice in the work of
his hand. If it pleases him to give good things, the soul is
grateful, but does not forget that the Giver is more than the
gift. If evil comes, pure love can quietly rest, desiring
naught for self, but all for him. Even if his face is hidden,
pure love, though feeling keenly the absence of its beloved,
can still say in sweet submission, "Thy will be done"; for it
feels itself unworthy of any blessing and so is content with

whatever its Lord is pleased to do. It yields itself to the Author of every good, and, trusting his love, receives thankfully and in deep humility what he pleases to give and as gratefully humbles itself to go without what he does not please to give. "Willingly to receive what thou givest, to lack what thou withholdest, to relinquish what thou takest, to suffer what thou inflictest, to be what thou requirest"— this is pure love and real consecration.

SEEING MY CONDITION

As God revealed this precious truth, I felt as though some one had said of me, "Doth Job serve God for naught?" and that God could not have justified me as he did Job. My own heart showed me self-seeking. I saw then that I had prayed to be blessed; that I had longed for satisfaction; that I had sought for joy and peace and love and spirituality, partly at least, that I might be satisfied and well pleased with myself, and, furthermore, that I might be considered spiritual among the brethren. Also, I was honestly anxious to be a blessing to others and in everything to be an "example of the believers." But to seek the Lord simply to please him never occurred to me, until I was reminded of his unselfish love for me. He desired me to be "all for him," not because my little all could make him any richer, but because it was only then that he could really be "all for me" and bestow upon me the riches of his love. A sentence from Fenelon made me more ashamed than ever. It reads something like this: "Would you serve God only as he gives you pleasure in serving him?"

LIGHT BREAKS UPON MY SOUL

In the beginning of my Christian experience I had but to see a truth to feel within a strong drawing to obedience. But now all was different. The cold facts of my condition were plain to me, but there was no inward force compelling me to act according to the knowledge I had gained. I was tossed about and wished more than I can tell for some inward urging of the Spirit of God toward the performance of my duty. I did not know the truth that God accepts the decision of the will as the purpose of the heart. I supposed that no act could be acceptable to God unless it came from a warm feeling of love. The deadness and the apathy of my heart were sickening. I saw clearly the wretchedness of my condition, but there was no breaking up, no feeling of sorrow, no conviction (as I thought), no love for God. If I could only have shed some tears; if my soul had only been exercised for its own deliverance! But all within was as still as a stone; only my mind seemed active.

At last, however, I saw that this apparent lack of sorrow was only another step toward the utter repudiation of self. In the past, self had hidden behind my tears, and I had unconsciously trusted in my sorrow instead of in the Lord, thinking that surely because I felt so sorry, I should not repeat the offense. But a feeling of sorrow can not save, as I proved again and again by repeated failures, and so God, wishing to strip me of anything in which to trust except himself, allowed me not even the satisfaction of tears or a breaking up of heart. He wished to teach me that real repentance is an act of the will and not of the emotions. For a tender heart, one should be grateful, but to trust in that for victory over sin or faults can only lead to repeated failure. So at last I was willing to submit this point to him who doeth all things well and was willing to cast myself, unworthy, undone, without a vestige of hope in myself, nor a place to set my feet, wholly upon him and to believe that he took me AS I WAS, whether I was able to do or be anything or not, and would begin to work in me his divine will.

LEARNING MY MISTAKES

The same trouble arose about my lack of feeling any love for God. How could I, who had been the recipient of so many favors from the hand of God, be so hard-hearted as not to love him! Could I dare come to him or ask anything from him when I did not love him, when I had given so much place to self-love and had been so indifferent concerning the pleasure of my King? How difficult it is to come to God empty-handed! If only I might have brought at least a little love in my hand to offer him! But no, there seemed to be none; and at last my poor soul came to see and confess that, after all, it was not because of my love to him that he loved me and saved me, but because of his great mercy and love for me. At length my soul, falling down before him, could cry out in truth,

"Nothing in my hand I bring;

Simply to thy cross I cling."

Then he taught me that love does not depend upon emotion; that so far as God is concerned, it is a free gift to us; that in order for us to enjoy it we must accept it as our own. The acceptance depends upon our will and decision in the matter, and not upon our feelings. To illustrate: If a person does much for me that is hard and difficult for him, willingly makes many sacrifices for me, without any hope of reward, I conclude that he loves me far better than the one who does much for me for which he receives or expects remuneration. Nowhere does the Bible command us to feel like obeying the Lord; nowhere is it even suggested that we should feel like loving him. But we do find that God's pleasure rests upon those who "will do his will" (John 7:17), and we do have this definition of love: "This is the love of God, that we keep his commandments." Feelings have nothing to do with the keeping of God's commands. Of course, it is more pleasant to us to do what we feel inclined to do, but it does not necessarily give more pleasure to God. If we obey God because he is God and because it is right to obey him, we act from pure love, and the pleasure God feels toward such service will in time be poured out upon the soul in streams of love, and there will be all the feeling desired.

Thus, I saw that if I willed to love God and acted as nearly as possible as I should act if I felt the glow of his love in my heart, this was more acceptable to him than the same service would be if rendered because my feelings prompted me to do it.

VICTORY OVER ACCUSATIONS

In acting upon this truth, I was often accused of being a hypocrite, because my prayers, my manifestations of love and interest in others, and whatever I did for the Lord, seemed unreal and strained. Here, however, faith came to my rescue, enabling me to say to Satan: "No, I am not a hypocrite. I know that I do not feel like doing what I am doing; I know that I am not getting any particular pleasure out of it. But I do not deserve any pleasure, and I shall continue to do the best I can to prove to God that I do love him and am trying to give him pleasure. If he never sees fit to give me back again the joy which I formerly had in his service, that is his business. Mine is to love and serve. Let him do as he will with his own."

It was all very dry and hard at first, for the old doubts about being his when I did not feel his presence, knocked hard for admittance; but I was enabled to meet them always with the same confidence: "I can not doubt that he loves me now, whether I seem to love him or not; for did he not 'love me and give himself for me' when I was not trying to serve him at all? Anyway, my salvation does not depend upon my love for him, but upon his for me. But I WILL love him and prove it by trusting and obeying him. This is all I can do; the rest I leave with him." The test was a long one, and a lesson that I shall not forget.

When, at last, God saw that I would ask only for ability to satisfy and please him, whether I felt pleased and satisfied or not, there came into my soul gradually light and joy, and oh! such a sweet sense of his presence. Praise his name! The love and other graces I then felt in my soul, I could not boast of, however, for they all came from and belonged to him; and when I was enabled again to bow before him with a sweet sense of love and reverence, I felt that in adoring and loving him, I was not bringing to him something of my own, but only returning to him that which he had given me. I felt as I had not for years that

"The graces within are not mine;

For the love and the power and the glory

Belong to the Savior divine."

LOCATING MYSELF SPIRITUALLY

One other point of which I must speak in this connection is the difficulty I experienced in endeavoring to locate myself spiritually when in the midst of the confusion I have described. Could I be saved at all when in such a state? Did I need to repent, or only try to do better? Were my careless actions and thoughtless words sins, or only mistakes? Fortunately, I was advised not to try to figure out so carefully what was sin and what was not, but to present to Jesus anything that troubled me, and to trust him implicitly to work in me the victory that I needed. By humbly confessing my weakness and claiming the promise of Phil. 2:13, "For it is God that worketh in you both to will and to do his good pleasure," I was enabled to gain victory almost immediately over many faults and failures with which I had wrestled long and over which I could never have gotten victory if I had spent my time picking every failure to pieces to find out whether it was something of which I needed to repent as a sin or only a mistake. I felt that God was pleased to have me humbly confess and trustingly turn over to him for correction any and every error whether it seemed to me serious or not.

It would take too much space to tell here of all the changes which were wrought in me by these experiences. Suffice it to say that life has been different ever since. Not that I have always felt the Lord just as near, for he has needed to remind me of the lessons I have recorded and to teach me others; but whether he seems near or far, Satan has never succeeded in making me fear and doubt. I have learned that whether God leads in light or in darkness, he IS leading and I have nothing to fear. If darkness comes upon me, it is for a purpose, and I can wait patiently upon him until he makes that purpose known. Submissively to wait and patiently to trust in him till he reveals his purposes is my part. His part is to lead and take care of me, and this, I am sure, he will do unto the end. Therefore I have no responsibility except to go on obeying and trusting him. Whatever bothers or troubles me in myself or others I lay at his feet, expecting him to give me victory if the trouble be in myself, or to bring it out in his own good way if it be in others. And thus my soul has reached and abides in that "wealthy place" where no harm can ever come and where the soul is kept in perfect peace.

Liberated from Faultfinding

EXPERIENCE NUMBER 14

For the glory of God and the encouragement of others I wish to testify against the evil of faultfinding. Soon after the beginning of my Christian experience, about twelve years ago, I was severely harassed by this adversary of my soul. So cunningly were my eyes blinded to my real condition that I was almost overwhelmed at times through the workings of this dangerous influence.

At times I would be almost free from it, but very much of the time I seemed to have a peculiar faculty of finding the mote in the eyes of others and was never aware of the beam in my own eye. I could see so much to pick at in some brethren that there was no time left for me to step aside and occasionally take myself into account and see myself as others saw me. I thought I could conduct some affairs over which others had charge, so much better than they were being conducted, that I was at times uncomfortable because I did not have a chance to show what I could do. It is needless to say that during the time that I was a prey to this wicked spirit, I had little, if any, spiritual life; but I tried to convince myself that I was doing quite well. There was, however, a blank or a real lack in my Christian life, because I had not learned to be an ideal Christian in humility before God and meekness towards my fellow men.

As soon as I passed through enough sad experiences to make me the happy possessor of a willing spirit, I began to realize that I was learning the necessary lessons and through these trials and tribulations I began to have a little understanding of the cause and root of my trouble.

There were three happenings that aided in awakening me to my need. The first one was a few years ago, when I received from a brother a letter in which he said, "Brother, you need continuity." That reproof found its place in my heart, and the first seed was sown toward a harvest of willingness. Although it brought no immediate results, yet it stayed by me and was very prominent before me many times.

The second lesson was brought to me through a sermon. The sister who delivered the sermon related the experience of a brother who had years of difficulty in regard to finding fault with others, and who finally concluded that the trouble was more with him than with those he criticized. I began to see my own case a little clearer, but I did not fully learn the lesson until sometime later.

My third lesson came in the following manner: A brother in whom I had some confidence came to my home and asked for a position, which I secured for him. We admitted him into our home for his comfort as well as for our pleasure spiritually, as we supposed he would be a help to us. It was not long, however, until it seemed there was nothing that escaped his faultfinding. He saw mountains of fault with us and our children. At last I saw in his case a picture of what I myself had done during the past, but I had banished from my life all thoughts of ever again being influenced by such a faultfinding spirit. Never before had I been able to see the picture of my former condition as I saw it when fully manifested in the life of this brother.

Although it had been my desire and no doubt his full intention to do what was right, nevertheless this evil habit, if I may call it such, had gained such a foothold in my life and in his life as to be a hindrance to our own spiritual progress and a stumbling-block in the way of others. This habit of faultfinding by those who are claiming to be children of God has caused them to wander from the true paths of righteousness into forbidden paths, and also to turn many others from the path that leads to everlasting life.

It is with much gratitude to God that I undertake to tell of my deliverance from that great barrier and hindrance to my spiritual progress. When I came to the point where I humbled my heart before the Lord and let him turn the searchlight upon me, the faults in others were not so great, but mine had seemed to climb mountain high. It was with a determination and positive decision to turn from such things; and the Lord, understanding my intentions in regard to those things, took note of my humility of heart and delivered me, for which I give him all the praise and glory. May the dear Lord help us all to bear with each other, and forbear complaining, even though it may at times seem necessary. I am sure it will bring about a great measure of the grace of God.

Help from God in Fiery Trials

EXPERIENCE NUMBER 15

When I think of the great mercy and love of God that follows after a soul and remember that he knows all about the thoughts and intents of the heart, truly I stand in awe before him. Since he knows all and has all power, can we not trust him when we give ourselves into his hands to be molded into his image to shine for him?

"Not every one that saith unto me, Lord, Lord, shall enter into the kingdom of heaven, but he that doeth the will of my Father." Every one who will give all into his hands will be brought through the fire, according to Zech. 13:9—"And I will bring a third part through the fire, and will refine them as silver is refined, and will try them as gold is tried: they shall call on my name, and I will hear them: I will say, It is my people: and they shall say, The Lord is my God." In telling some experiences in the furnace-flames, I wish to lose sight of everything except to be a help and encouragement to those who are in trial.

In writing my experience, I shall find it necessary to make mention of some of the sad things concerning my husband, a fact which I very much regret. But I trust that dear souls will take warning and realize that there is no limit to the work of the enemy when once he gains possession. I shall never cease to be thankful for the first copies of a paper called the Gospel Trumpet I ever saw. Through my reading them, conviction was sent to my soul by the Spirit of God; but being unwilling to meet the necessary conditions, I resisted the convictions and put the papers aside.

Some months afterwards while searching for something, I came across those papers, and immediately that same conviction returned, but again I resisted it. My health failed, and I continued to decline until I was almost in the jaws of death. Physicians could do nothing for me. During this time God was doing his best to get me to understand that if I would give up he would save and heal me. At last I yielded, and he saved my soul and healed me, and from that day until this, which has been more than eighteen years, I have been fascinated by the charms of a Christian life.

THE BEGINNING OF PERSECUTIONS

For a long time I did not meet with any persecution in my home, as my husband saw the light of the gospel and believed it to be the truth, but was not willing to walk in it. God followed after him with love and long-suffering. Time after time he resisted the conviction, but finally the Spirit succeeded in breaking up his heart and showed him what he must do to make his wrongs right. He began making a profession of religion, but refused to make all his wrongs right, and in a short time the enemy took possession of him, whereupon he turned against God and against me, and grew worse and worse.

Now the furnace-flames became hot. He was restless and could not be content to stay anywhere very long at a time, and everywhere we went he set about to turn the people against me by telling untruths to gain sympathy. He was very cruel to the children and me.

After we moved to a small town in northern Kansas, these words came vividly to my mind: "Fear none of those things which shall come upon thee." With the cruelty and persecution came a severe affliction. Two doctors pronounced it tuberculosis in the knee-joint. It was so serious that I could not bear to be moved, and when I sat in a rocking-chair I was obliged to have something under the rocker to keep the chair from moving. The thoughts of any one's coming near my knee made the pains go through my limb. At times I was able to walk some on crutches by being careful. My leg was swollen from above the knee down. At night I had to lie upon my back with pillows under my knee, and I could move neither to the right nor to the left, and sometimes just to cough a little caused almost unendurable pain.

All this happened during the months before a baby girl was born. My family and neighbors did not expect me to live, but God stood by me and gave me this assurance: that as the children of Israel faced the Red Sea with no possible way of crossing, and he divided the waters and let them pass through, so he would in like manner help me. Oh, it was precious to trust him!

Just about a week before the child was born, the excruciating pain left my knee, but upon my recovery it came back seemingly worse than ever. About three months later the Lord healed the disease, which has never returned.

However, I was left a cripple, and have had to use crutches ever since that time.

At this time I had eight children. Two grown boys had gone from home, leaving me to care for the other six. I had a great desire to rear them for God. Thus far I had spent most of my Christian life in isolated places, where I was deprived of church privileges. It seemed that all the hosts of darkness were united against my determination to rear my children under Christian influence. Although I had many things to learn regarding how to do this, yet God was patient in teaching me.

Once when an awful discouragement tried to settle down over me, and it seemed there was no material to work on, I was comforted through the impression that came to me in the words, "God can take a worm and thresh a mountain," and I have never forgotten these words, the thought of which is expressed by the prophet in Isa. 41:14, 15. I felt that some who opposed me would be glad for me to die so that they could get the children from my influence. Once my husband was threatened with arrest for cruelty, and I feared that my children would be taken from me and placed among my opposers, as one woman had said there were plenty of homes for them. Then the scene of Christ before Pilate came before me and this scripture: "Thou couldest have no power at all against me, except it were given thee from above." At the same time one of the organ-keys was down, and we were unable to repair it; so I said, "We will trust the Lord to fix it." When the above-mentioned scripture came to me, the organ-key raised of its own accord, and I said, "Is there anything like that in the Bible?" and quickly came the answer: "The gate opened of its own accord when Peter went out." Joy filled my soul as I realized that the mighty God of heaven was my helper.

At another time I made a carpet which required five years to make by working whenever I could find time to do so. After it was finished and before I had cut it, the Spirit said to me, while I was praying one day, "Send that carpet to Kansas City to help furnish the Missionary Home." My heart said amen, and God made my husband willing, blessed my soul in sending it, and later gave me a carpet larger than the one I had given. My husband had ceased to allow me to have a way to make money of my own. I was not permitted to have either chickens or eggs. Once I made a hot-bed, as plants found a ready sale, and thought I would make a little money in that way, but he found it just as the plants were coming up and destroyed it. God never failed to bless me when I said amen.

At one time when I was in need of a pair of shoes, I went in earnest prayer to the Lord like a child and asked him for a pair. Soon afterwards I received a letter from a sister in Kansas City whom I had never seen. She was giving her entire time to the gospel work and had a little money in her possession. In her letter she said, "My mind was directed to you last Sunday during the services, and I was impressed to send this money to you." At another time after praying for some money, I received a dollar. I was in need of so many things that I asked the Lord how I should spend it. This answer came: "Send it to the missionaries in India." I did so, and in a short time received three pair of shoes for the children, of which they were very much in need. I had many similar experiences.

When our baby girl was about three months old, a dear sister whom I had met and who was living in an isolated place, came to pay me a visit. She remained in that community. After about a year she was eager to grow in grace, and while she was anxiously waiting before the Lord and wishing that she might grow like Sister ———, the question came to her, "Are you willing to pass through what she has had to pass through?" She had a desire to do whatever was necessary, but did not feel that she could very well pass through such severe ordeals. In order to be spiritual and grow in grace, it is not always necessary for people to pass through such severe trials, nevertheless their consecration must be to pass through anything that would be most to the glory of God.

About this time I had an attack of sickness, and for sometime it seemed that I might die. My husband went to visit his sister and left me alone with the children. The sister who had been staying in the community, felt that she must come and stay with me, and when my husband returned, the Lord put it into his heart to hire her for a while. The Lord healed me and made my husband willing for my oldest daughter and I to go to a meeting at Kansas City. This was my last opportunity to enjoy a meeting before entering a much darker vale of trial. Our daughter was saved, for which I praised the Lord. My husband refused to hire the sister any longer, but in answer to prayer consented for her to stay as long as she desired without pay for her services.

In December of that year a dear baby boy was born. The Lord gave me this assurance: "I will be with thee in six troubles, yea, in seven there shall no evil befall thee." My husband began planning to go to Arkansas. We had been here three years and were getting our home comfortably furnished, but we learned to take joyfully the spoiling of our goods and to see them sold at a great sacrifice.

One day while I was communing with the Lord, this scripture was vividly impressed upon my mind: "In all thy ways acknowledge him, and he shall direct thy paths." At that time there was suggested to my mind the name of a town in Kansas near where I lived during my childhood. I did not understand what it meant, as we did not go there, but I understood later. I had always had an aversion to living in the backwoods, for I knew that the welfare and education of the children would be neglected, but I acknowledged God's way.

The sister who was with us was willing to stay or go with us. We asked the Lord to open the way if he wanted her to go, and my husband told her that if she wanted to go he would pay her way. There are many experiences through which I passed that I should like to relate—experiences showing the mysterious ways in which the Lord helped us in time of need. I learned that obedience and trueness to God will bring us into a wealthy place.

My husband went about six weeks before we did and secured a location. Upon our arrival we found that our home for the present was sixteen miles from a railroad, back in the mountains, and that the roads were very rough and rocky. Our house was a very small one built of rough, unhewn logs. There were no windows, only some small shutters which could be opened when the weather was not cold. There were plenty of cracks and the fireplace was a smoky one. Most of the people in that community had lived there from the time of their birth and were poor. The women used tobacco. Some could not read, and morality was at a low ebb.

Soon after being introduced to our new surroundings, I was asked these three questions in succession:

"Are you willing to stay here and work?"

"Yes," I answered.

"Unseen and unknown?"

"Yes."

"Not even an obituary when you die?"

"Yes."

There were only twenty acres in cultivation, which required more hard work than eighty acres of ordinary farm-land. That fall my husband purchased a hewed log house of three rooms and moved it down between the mountains. It had four whole windows and two half windows, and we never knew before what luxuries they were.

We continued to have Sunday-school, as husband had not yet forbidden us to have it. He succeeded in turning most of the people against us by telling the usual stories, only he changed them to suit the people. He often used the same whip for the children and me that he used for the horses. His condition grew worse and worse all the time. The second summer three of the children had typhoid fever. After the first one had been ill for nine days, we sent for a doctor according to the law. He said, "Your little girl has a straight case of typhoid well developed, and it will take twenty-one days for the fever to break, with the best of care, if she lives at all." I told him that my trust was in God, but he ignored what I said. My husband told him to leave medicine and ordered me to give it, not because he had no confidence in divine healing, but for fear of the law, and to please the people. She had never taken a dose of medicine in her life and wanted to trust the Lord. I submitted and gave a few doses. God had given me witness that he would heal her, and in three days she was sitting up and was soon up. My husband was very angry because she was healed. About two weeks later she took a relapse and was seemingly worse than ever, but we trusted in the promise, and she was soon all right again. Then two of the others contracted the disease, but they were both healed in answer to prayer.

One day during the summer while I was in the timber praying, a vivid impression came to me that God was going to deliver us out of that place, and the name of the town where we should live was given me. This was the same town previously mentioned, near where I had lived during my childhood. Oh, such rapture filled my soul! I told my daughter, and she said the Lord had been showing her the same thing. This scripture was given to me: "I know the thoughts that I think toward you, saith the Lord, thoughts of peace, and not of evil, to give you an expected end. And I will be found of you, saith the Lord; and I will turn away your captivity" (Jer. 29:11, 14).

We had never sent the children to school here, as the people were so poor and of such a low grade morally. I taught our children during the winter. At the end of the second summer we began praying for shoes. One day the children came from the mail-box with a pair for my oldest daughter, and then in a few days a letter came from an unsaved woman whom I had never met. She said: "I have some money from the Lord and feel impressed to send it to you. Please write and tell me how to send it." Then we received from a sister a letter containing five dollars. We had already begun to get ready to go to our future home. We had a catalog, from which we ordered as God gave us the means, and seldom my husband knew anything about it, for he would not have wanted us to have the money had he known it. He seldom noticed how much sewing was going on.

The Lord in many ways encouraged our hearts, for there were fiery trials awaiting us. A neighbor had moved away and hired my husband to dig his potatoes and sweet potatoes. The enemy had such control of my husband that he could not be honest. My daughter helped to dig them, and he told her not to take any pains to get them all, but she did her best. He brought nearly half a bushel of sweet potatoes home and told me to cook them. I prayed to know what to do and received these words, "He that sweareth to his own hurt and changeth not." I told my husband that it was not right to keep the potatoes and that I could not cook them. He flew into a rage and threatened to kill me, and would not allow me to come into the room where the rest were until the light was out and they had gone to bed. It seemed the enemy and all his hosts wanted to take my life. I cried earnestly unto the Lord to give me something to comfort my soul, and he brought to my mind the three Hebrew children.

A week passed and the man returned for some of his belongings. It was dark when he passed, and he was drunk. My husband went out and talked, and no doubt smoothed it over about the sweet potatoes. When he came back, he said to me, "I told you it was all right about those potatoes." I did not say anything, but did not feel right about it. The next morning before daylight, he wanted me to cook those potatoes. I refused and told him I could not cook them. Then the battle was on worse than ever. He struck me and wanted me to leave the house, and followed me with a club until I was outside the yard, and then told me to move on. I went out into the timber and remained there, and the children brought me some wraps and something to eat. Then he ordered the sister who was with us to leave, and she packed a few clothes in a suit-case and came down the timber to see me. We parted in good courage. This sister had, before this happened, received many calls to go elsewhere. One call was from her brother, who offered her a good home and support during the rest of her life.

She went to a neighbor who had given her an invitation and stayed two days, and from there to another place, where she stayed a few days and worked for her board. While she was on the way, the Lord gave her this assurance: "Trust in the Lord, and thou shalt be fed." While she was there, not knowing what to do next, and being taunted by the enemy because she had not accepted her brother's offer, the Lord seemed sweetly to whisper to her, these words: "This is the way; walk ye in it."

She heard of a place where they might need some one. It was very muddy and there was a drizzling rain, but she went. When she arrived at that place, she found they did not need her, but the telephone rang, and a lady who had been one of our opposers asked that she come and stay with her for a while. The scripture had come to her, "Inasmuch as ye have done it unto one of the least of these my brethren, ye have done it unto me." The woman turned friend, opened the way for her to communicate with us and to get mail from the people of God. She remained there about a week, when an old lady desired some one to stay with her and gave her a home until the Lord was through with her in Arkansas.

But returning to my experience in the timber, I did not know whether I should be allowed to return home or not; but trusting God, I returned in the afternoon and was not molested, excepting a tongue-lashing. Not long after this our two grown sons came home on a visit, and my husband told them awful things about me, which they believed, and turned against me and doubled the persecution. They searched the house for books, Bibles, and papers, and burned them before us, also pictures of our friends. Then they tortured the little girls, trying to make them promise that they would not be Christians like their mother. Those dear boys who had stood by me in the past! How I thanked God for grace sufficient in time of trial and for the privilege of loving and praying for them.

In July of our last summer there, my eldest daughter said, "I just feel like packing my trunk to go to ———." It was the town God had shown us should be our home. The next time she went for the mail, there was a letter from a sister in the town, saying that God had taken sleep from two sisters and told them to send for her, and enclosed a check for her fare. She soon afterward went to that town.

Sometime after this, while the second daughter was driving for her father while husking corn, she ran into a stump and broke the wagon-tongue. Such an occurrence endangered their lives, but two men coming along just at that time spared her somewhat, and her father sent her to the house. I prayed until my faith rested on the promise for protection. That night after I had gone to bed, God inspired me with beautiful thoughts of heaven, and I got up so softly and took a pencil and paper and wrote this poem in the dark. I can not refrain from saying here, Praise the Lord for these precious things in time of trial!

MY BEAUTIFUL HOME

Though poets may sing of the streets of pure gold

And talk of its mansions so fair,

After all it is naught; the half is not told

Of my beautiful home over there.

Man's eye has ne'er seen nor his ear ever heard,

Nor can he e'er picture the scene;

The music's so rare no one can record

The strains of the faithful, I ween.

Though art has portrayed fair angels of light

In tints that enrapture the mind;

'Tis grander by far in my home ever bright,

Where the glory of God is enshrined.

No; ear hath not heard, and eye hath not seen,

Any thing that will ever compare

With the grandeur and beauty of that heavenly scene,

Of my beautiful home over there.

'Tis only by faith that gleams from the land,

Where they need not the light of the sun,

Can brighten the life or lighten the pain

Of those who will hear the "Well done."

Some day when my toiling and trials are o'er,

I shall see the fair angels of light;

On their wings they will bear me across to that shore

Where my faith will be lost in the sight.

On the night of November 22 the children and I were alone, and I was wonderfully impressed with the scripture in Isa. 45:2, 3. It came to me three times during the day. The next morning, being Sunday, we were still alone. The children were singing "What a Mighty God We Serve," when I heard a crackling noise and, looking up, saw the house was on fire. I looked to the Lord for presence of mind, and we went to work getting things out. One of the children said, "This is what your scripture was for. Perhaps this is for our deliverance." I realized the presence of the Lord in the whole affair, and he wonderfully helped us to save all the things of importance, and just as the fire was getting so hot that it seemed we could do no more, a man came along and helped us. There was an empty house nearby, into which we moved.

The people decided to help my husband build another house, and they began work. Thus, it appeared that we should have to remain there always; but the children and I took no notice of it. I told the Lord he knew there was more clothing we needed yet, and asked him, to give me, when it was time, the money to get the goods. In a short time I received it, and we were busy sewing until late at night, and the Lord gave me such a glorious assurance of deliverance.

I had two trunks packed full, mostly with clothing. Husband said one day, "I believe I will trade the place." I did not know what to say, as I knew God was doing the managing. In a few days he traded it and decided to go about twenty miles north and rent some land. This was about the first of February, and he wanted to start in March. The man who owned the house where we were living, came and wanted it, and so we put up a small tent to live in the rest of the time. It began raining and rained hard the most of the time for two or three weeks. Everything was so damp, but God's hallowed presence made all things bearable.

My husband planned to take two teams and have me drive one. I knew almost nothing about driving, and the roads were as bad as they could be, up and down mountains, over rocks, and through mud, and I could scarcely make a move of any kind to please my husband. He also decided to take twenty-nine goats, which he intended having the children drive. The morning we started I had been sick all night, and it began raining and the wagon sheet began to leak; but I kept trusting, and it stopped raining. Our first interesting experience was the horses balking in the river. It took about an hour before we got out. No damage was done, however, except that Husband found a roll of papers which I had intended for distribution, and threw them into the river.

We camped near a house that night. The next morning Husband said, "Unpack that box and leave the dishes here, for we are too heavily loaded." The box had been packed with care and contained some of my best things, and about two sets of dishes which had scarcely been used. He left them with some other things. One of the girls who had walked the day before became ill. We started on our way up a mountain slope, which was a distance of three miles. After we had gone a short distance, my husband said, "I am going back and unload some of these things." He proceeded to throw out the bedding and other things on the wet ground and, leaving us, went back and left the trunks with the dishes. Both trunks were unlocked and there were so many people who could not be trusted. I had taken the address of the people with whom I left the dishes. We had no clothing left except what we had on our persons, and a few things I had felt impressed to keep out before we left home. The trunks contained all the clothing for our future home, so I believed that God would take care of them.

The roads could not have been worse nor more dangerous. Some places were so steep and one-sided that it seemed the wagon might fall over, and the mud-holes were terrible. The team which I was driving gave much trouble, as one mule pulled ahead and the other was slow. Husband expected me to keep them even and drive with one hand, and he quite often gave me a lick with the same club with which he whipped the mules. Two of the children were sick, and the jolts of the wagon were very hard on them. While passing through some of these experiences, the words of Paul came to me, "In perils often; a night and a day have I been in the deep," and the song, "Anywhere with Jesus I Can Safely Go." I must say, Praise the Lord, for he helped my faith to rise above the situation and healed the children and protected our lives.

My husband failed to find any land to rent or work, so we kept going. Two of the children were still walking and driving the goats. On account of the limited space I can tell but very little of their experiences along the way. One circumstance, however, that gave us much concern was that there were many streams to cross, and at one place by driving the goats along on the mountain-side the children would miss having to cross the stream several times, and they were required to take the mountain-side. It was steep and above the river. Sometimes they would slide and have considerable difficulty in stopping, and the goats would run up the mountains, jump on rocks, and cause trouble. My husband drove on and would not wait for them at the bridge, which was about a mile from where they started, and it was some time before I saw them again, a time of great anxiety. It was one of the times when I had to trust the Lord to take care of them.

After the children had driven the goats about two weeks, my husband sold them. One day about four weeks after we left our home, I heard my husband tell a man that he was going to ———. This was the town the Lord had shown me would be our future home. You will remember that our clothing was left behind, so that our appearance was not presentable; but I deepened my consecration and told the Lord that if he wanted us to go in such a plight, I could say amen. Before we arrived, he opened the way for us so that we looked quite presentable, considering the fact that we were traveling. A week before our arrival, I wrote for the trunks to be sent to the town. We arrived in safety. Three weeks after I wrote for our goods, they had not arrived, and so I wrote again. We received a letter from the people saying that they had moved and left the trunks in the house, which was not locked. We gave them the dishes and other things in order to get them to take the goods to the railroad, and upon the arrival of the trunks we found them just as I had packed them.

We were now glad to be with the dear people of God and to know that the captivity was turned. My husband began telling the usual stories, but they were not received even by his own people. He became very miserable and alarmed about his own safety on account of the people. He left the town, and has never been heard from. During these years of trial, many hours of deep concern have been spent with a hope and trust that the dark shades which cover his life may be swept away and that even yet his future life here on earth may be crowned with the blessings of the Lord and the presence of the Almighty. I do not know what the future holds in store, but I am expecting some good things from God, whether or not my pathway is strewn with trials.

In relating this experience, I have been obliged to omit many things that could have been told and that might have been helpful to others who are passing through similar trials, as there are so many experiences that would not be advisable to publish. I believe that the good part may be a help and encouragement to many who have like trials and that the sad experiences may be a warning to those who trifle with the mercy of God. My dear husband might have been with us and happy today instead of suffering an awful foretaste of the regions of the lost, had he only been obedient to the Lord and walked in the light of his Word. The sister who was in Arkansas is with us, and we are working together for the Lord.

I have humbly submitted everything into the hands of the Lord and have been better able to understand the words of the Psalmist, wherein he said, "Teach me thy way, 0 Lord, and lead me in a plain path, because of mine enemies. Deliver me not over unto the will of mine enemies: for false witnesses are risen up against me, and such as breathe out cruelty. I had fainted, unless I had believed to see the goodness of the Lord in the land of the living. Wait on the Lord: be of good courage, and he shall strengthen thine heart: wait, I say, on the Lord."

Experience of a School-Teacher in India

EXPERIENCE NUMBER 16

The message of the cross is the same in every clime. The Spirit of the Lord will enlighten all darkened hearts that are receptive to the truth.

In the year 1904 there was a striking occurrence in one of our meetings in the Punjab district in northwestern India. An intelligent young lady, a native school-teacher, offered her services as interpreter one Sunday while I preached on the subject of the ordinances of the Bible.

She became very much interested in the story of the cross, and as the prophecy was read from the fifty-third chapter of Isaiah, she was much affected. After interpreting sentence by sentence a vivid description of the crucifixion-scene and the story of how the Savior gave his life for the salvation of those who are lost in sin, she suddenly stopped, began wringing her hands, and fell upon her knees. In the bitter anguish of her soul she cried, "O Lord! I am a sinner! I am a sinner! Have mercy upon my soul!"

For a few minutes the services changed to a prayer-meeting. Her efforts were with such earnestness and sincerity of heart that she was soon able to realize a fulfilment of the promises by faith, and received a witness to her soul that the Lord Jesus was now her Savior.

She arose rejoicing and continued to interpret with much fervency of spirit, realizing the truthfulness of the words of the apostle when he said that the gospel of Christ "is the power of God unto salvation to every one that believeth."

Unconquered Will Won by Love

EXPERIENCE NUMBER 17

"Some feet there be which walk life's track unwounded,

Which find but pleasant ways,

But they are few. Far more there are who wander

Without a hope or friends;

Who find their journey full of pains and losses,

And long to reach the end."

Yet if, like Elisha's servant, we could open our blind
spiritual eyes, how often we might discover myriads of
angels waiting only for a submissive spirit and a
surrendered will to plant such feet upon substantial ways of
blessings and courage instead of the ways of the wounds
and thorns and crosses. If I had but the power to tell of
some such experiences of my own, I feel it might
encourage some other soul to surrender fully to God a life
that otherwise has been a failure. There is no doubt that
God has ministering servants ever ready to wait on the soul
that surrenders to his will. The difficulty is always the
unsurrendered will.

When I was about fourteen years old, an evangelist came to
our town to preach a full salvation, one that saves from sin
and sanctifies the soul. The Holy Spirit was working in

many hearts. One evening as I was riding home facing the west at sunset, I beheld, in the shifting of the clouds, a huge black cross. It stood there between me and the sun. I thought of Jesus dying on the cross, and that seemed very fitting, though of course very sad. As this cross remained there, it impressed me more solemnly, until I began to realize that there might be a cross for me also. But I said: "Life is what we make it. I do not want crosses; I choose other things." At last a gorgeous crown of the sunset enveloped the cross, and in my heart I knew that without the cross there would be no crown. The difficulty had arisen between me and God. His ministering servants were ready to spare me the "pains and losses," but my will was not surrendered. I would not bear the cross.

Another warning came to me a few nights later, when I was invited to the home of a friend to attend a dance. I thought of the meeting and its solemn significance, and felt uneasy about going. I wanted to please Jesus, who had borne the cross for me, but I justified myself in going because the crowd was select. I went to my room thus battling with my conscience. I knelt as in prayer and soon felt what seemed unmistakably to be the presence of some one in my room. I looked up, and it seemed that I could see the smiling face of Jesus. Sweetness filled my soul, and the room was full of joy. All earthly pleasures faded away. I had no desire for anything now but this captivating Jesus. My heart was enraptured. Christ, I realized then, was sufficient.

This, you see, was given that I might understand how Christ might make all crosses easy to bear. To be sure, this impression sank deep, and I have never forgotten it, but my will was yet unsurrendered and unconquered. I would not come when called in sweetest tones. In a "journey full of pains and losses," "without hope or friends," I walked life's track. God did not have his way, but I had mine. Often, so often in the years that followed I remembered the last night of the revival that had brought to my mind such serious thoughts. At the close of the last sermon a gospel worker came directly to me. I was confused. I had not decided what to do. I did not want to cast my lot with these people; I wanted to join a more fashionable church. As she approached me, I whispered to her, "I am going to join the other church." She said, "Be sure your heart is right," but I was not sure.

Perhaps if I had had more teaching about surrendering my will to God, I would have yielded and in this way avoided the powers of hell that laid hold upon me from that time. I was powerless in the hands of these unseen foes. Everything went against me. My life was ruined. There was no hope. Despair was my companion for years. Sickness and disease possessed my body, and sin became my hated master.

"Could we but draw back the curtains

That surround each other's lives,

See the naked heart and spirit—ah, if we only could!

"If we knew—alas! and do we

Ever care to know

Whether bitter herbs or roses

In our neighbor's garden grow?"

I attended many churches, heard many noted preachers, my soul suffering the while from awful convictions and desires for a higher life, but without a ray of light. After years of suffering I finally discerned that what was necessary was to make a complete surrender of myself to God. This I did with all my heart, hesitating no longer to bear any cross he saw fit to send. I made a full surrender, and God gave me salvation. At this time I had great need of spiritual advice; for I was so ignorant of the laws of salvation that I did not know that when God had taken away my burden of sin and washed me clean and made my heart feel so new and light and happy, he had made me his child. I knew about as much concerning spiritual things as a heathen. At last, a very dear, good woman became a mother to me. She was the first person who ever asked me about my soul. She taught me to talk about spiritual things and to understand them. She taught me the lessons of truth from God's own Word. She showed me by God's Word how I might live entirely free from the blight of sin, how I might dress and eat and live to his glory. It was all very new, but it was all more pleasant than the choicest food I had ever tasted. She taught me that by his Word and promises he was able and willing to heal my mortal body. Physicians said my case was hopeless and that I could live but a short time. I did not care to live until God showed me I might live for others. Then I was ready to bear my cross and God was ready to plant my feet on solid ground away from the "pains and losses" that brought grief and misery to my life. Blessings now fell upon my pathway. When fever fastened itself upon me and my body was being rapidly consumed by its fires, God instantly raised me up. He caused me to "forget the things of the past and press on."

"Whilst thou wouldst only weep and bow,

He said, 'Arise and shine!'"

He has given me a life victorious. He gave me a companion and little children and over every adversity, sickness, and misunderstanding he makes me victor. When my little girl lost her eyesight and became blind, the Lord healed her in answer to prayer and restored her sight in an instant. Time and space fail me to tell of the victorious incidents of this blessed life that comes from surrendering a will to God. Ah, that he might have fulfilled his purpose in the beginning! It was not his will that I should suffer.

"Can we think that it pleases his loving heart

To cause us a moment's pain?

Ah no, but he saw through the present cross

The bliss of eternal gain."

An Experience a Hundred Years Ago

EXPERIENCE NUMBER 18

I have often thought of recording some of the mercies of my God—the experience of his goodness to my soul. I was fond of the gaieties and follies of the world until about fifteen years of age, when I became awakened to the needs of my soul. In all former seasons when God called me, I was unwilling to part with the vanities of the world or to bear the reproach of the cross. I wanted the Christian's safety without his duties and crosses, but I now fell at the Savior's feet and inquired with trembling, anxious words: "Lord, what shall I do? I will part with everything or do anything for an interest in Jesus."

I do not recollect deep conviction for any particular sin, but sorrow that I had lived so long in neglect of God, not being willing to acquaint myself with him who is the fountain of all blessedness. I did not obtain an evidence of pardon and acceptance for about three weeks, though I sought it with prayer and tears. My burden had become exceeding heavy, too heavy for my strength, and I sank to the floor. While kneeling there I was absorbed in contemplation of the glories of the heavenly world. In an instant darkness, sorrow, and mourning fled away, and peace unspeakable and full of glory took their place. I rose to my feet to sing and rejoice in the name of my dear Redeemer.

I was away from home with a family who were not Christians, though amiable, kind friends. I said nothing to them, but they had noticed my distress and now observed the happy change. Among my private writings I find the transaction thus recorded:

"January 13, 1805.—I have this day publicly devoted myself to the service of God and entered into a solemn covenant with the eternal King of heaven to renounce the sinful pleasures of the world, with whatever is displeasing in his pure and holy eyes; to walk in his commandments and ordinances; to seek his glory and the best interests of his church here below; and in confidence of well-doing, to look forward to a happy inheritance with the saints in light."

For a season I thought I was dead to the world, but did not persevere in that course of consecration, which alone secures unwavering hope. As I was the only young person in the neighborhood who professed religion amid a large society, naturally amiable and loved, I had many temptations to return to folly, which I mainly resisted; but sometimes I went with them instead of endeavoring to bring them all to Christ. Here I first experienced a diminution of my happiness. I could not go from the circle of my folly to my closet and find my Savior and hold sweet communion with him, but with adoring wonder, I remember that when I repented, he forgave me. When I returned to him, he healed my backslidings and loved me freely.

After I was married, I was anxious to train my children in the ways of the Lord, but through many cares and on account of having to work very hard, I neglected their early religious instruction. I found that I needed a deeper work of grace in my heart, and when for the time I ought to be a teacher, I had need that one teach me again the first principles of the oracles of God. My prayer was, "Create in me a clean heart, O God, and renew a right spirit within me." I wanted to be freed from sin and thoroughly cleansed from all iniquity, so that I should never vex or grieve him more.

For something more than a year I suffered much from the buffetings and temptations of Satan. I knew that Jesus was near and sustained me in those conflicts, although it seemed that he had left me alone to contend with the powers of darkness. In the midst of these trials I had temptations of rebellion against God to call him unjust, to reproach him for creating me. The temptations came to "contradict him." I did it, but oh, the horror of that moment!

Until then I had resisted every temptation, as I thought, but now a worm crushed to the earth beneath the mountain weight of its sins had dared to rise in the face of infinite wisdom and excellence and contradict him. This, I thought, must be the sin for which there is no forgiveness. But I could weep tears of penitence; could sink at his feet and own it just. What less could his insulted majesty and purity do than crush the rebel worm! But he did not do it. Not even a frown was upon his gracious brow. It seemed that there was salvation for every sinner who had not, like me, contradicted him and thereby made him a liar. I contemplated the glorious character of God and concluded that unless I could find evidence that my sin was against the Holy Ghost, I should only be repeating that dreadful sin while I refused to believe the promises intended for me when penitent.

I retired with my Bible spread open before me and, kneeling down, read and prayed over the chapters in Hebrews which represent the blessed Savior as our sacrifice and high priest. In the twenty-fifth verse of the seventh chapter I found this assurance: "He is able to save them to the uttermost that come unto God by him, seeing he ever liveth to make intercession for them." Here was something to meet my case. "To the uttermost" I had insulted him, but "to the uttermost" he could save. I believed and here my soul entered into rest. I embraced the promises, rich and boundless, as my own. In Christ Jesus they are all there for me. I felt and said with heaven-born confidence, "This is firm footing; this is solid rock. My feet are placed upon it to remove no more." The view was not transporting or rapturous like my first conversion (if so it may be called), but calm, delightful, "strong consolation," firmer than the everlasting hills because founded on the immutable Word and oath of God in Christ. It was "hope as an anchor to the soul, both sure and stedfast, and which entereth into that within the veil."

Eleven years have passed since, and my peace has been like a river. In the world, to be sure, I have had tribulation and expect to have, for Jesus told me I should; but, blessed be his name! in him I have peace. I love the subject of Christian perfection, or entire sanctification in this life; but I have not been fully able to reach the point to obtain that deeper experience. Yet I believe I perfectly desire to do the will of God. May God bless the efforts of all dear brethren who are laboring to promote the sanctification of believers.

An Indian Mother's Submission

EXPERIENCE NUMBER 19

To show that God works the same in the hearts of his people wherever they are, I wish to mention the experience of one of my Indian sisters. Her little son contracted enteric fever. Every possible aid was given him, but he continued to grow worse. The fever caused him to become unconscious at intervals. The parents then decided to remove him to a hospital, that he might have skilled attention. Soon after being taken to the hospital, he became entirely unconscious, in which condition he remained for weeks, yes, for months. He was unable to take nourishment in the natural way and became a wonder to all who came to see him, as he was at the point of death yet did not die. Many who were not acquainted with the parents, but heard of the case, went to the hospital to see him.

The father and mother spent as much time as possible at the hospital, but when weeks and months had passed, they gave up hope for his recovery. All the Christians who knew of this child's sickness were praying for him and felt that God only could restore him to health. The parents knew a man who believed in divine healing and called him, and he anointed the child and prayed for him. He became so sick that the doctor thought he would not live until morning, and asked the parents to remain at the hospital that night.

The next day the father and mother went for a walk together, and while out walking he said to her, "We must become reconciled to losing our child, for it seems God is going to take him." At first the mother-heart could not yield to giving up the child, but at last she became resigned. Soon after this the child regained consciousness, but was weak, and his mind was almost a blank. He was like a new-born babe and had to learn to speak, although he was about nine years of age. Some thought he would never be normal again, and others thought he would be crippled. Since he has been restored to health, when that mother sees him enjoying the right use of his faculties and limbs, her heart is filled with thankfulness and praise to God.

She told me that the affliction of their child was a means of drawing their hearts closer to the Lord, and of enabling her to experience the sweet rest of being fully submitted to God, whereby she was afterwards able to teach others the way.

Just before this she had been urging a bereaved friend, who was grieving too much over the loss of her father, to become resigned to the will of God. Her friend said, "You can not appreciate my loss, for you have never suffered such a loss." She saw the force of her friend's remark and said no more. But when the affliction came upon her child and she was called upon to become resigned to the will of God, she came to know not only that it is possible to be resigned but that there is a great consolation in being submissive. When her friend afterwards came to know of her submission, she was very much affected.

Both my friend and her husband feel that God has given them their child from the grave, and their testimony is that through this severe ordeal they have come to love their Savior more.

The Conversion of My Father

EXPERIENCE NUMBER 20

The most precious experience in my life, I believe, next to my own conversion, was the salvation of my own dear father, for whom I had prayed a year and a half. He joined the Baptist denomination when only a young man, but, not having the real witness of sins forgiven, never felt satisfied with his Christian experience, or rather his profession. A few years later, feeling that he would be acting a hypocrite to go on in that condition, he even dropped his profession.

Eighteen or twenty years ago he attended a revival held by the United Brethren people and began to seek God. Night after night he went forward for prayer, but for lack of proper instruction, failed to find the peace he so earnestly sought.

A DISCOURAGEMENT

One day in this great soul-struggle, he called at the home of one of the ministers to know just how to get rid of the great load of sins he was carrying. He was completely baffled and disappointed. The minister said: "It is like this: A man might be carrying a heavy sack of sand upon his shoulders, and if for some reason there should come a little hole in the bottom of the sack and the sand begin to escape, it would leak out so slowly that it would be sometime before the burdened man would realize any difference in the weight of his load, and only in the end, after it had all slipped through a little hole, would he awaken to the fact that the entire load was gone. Now, just so it is with your burden of sins. As you begin to seek God, they begin to run out, but you will not realize any change at first, and it will take some time for you to realize that your load of guilt is really gone after you are fully forgiven."

Poor father! He turned away sick at heart, for he longed for an instantaneous work to be done in his soul. Through this discouragement he gave up trying to find God and for many years continued in that unhappy, dissatisfied state of soul and mind, although he often desired to be a true Christian for the sake of his family as well as for his own peace of mind, and yearned to be able to "read his title clear to mansions in the sky."

In the spring of 1906 his brother and family came to make us a short visit before their departure from the homeland as missionaries to a foreign country. For some months they had been especially burdened that at least one of our relatives should be saved before they crossed the ocean to their mission field. Their pure, holy lives made a deep impression upon me, and through their earnest prayers and fastings for my poor soul, I was constrained to forsake sin and yield myself to the Lord. I was glad to embrace the privilege of being with the humble people of God who worship him in spirit and in truth, and to become one of them. I had a feeling, however, that my father might be displeased with me for making such a decision; but when I met him a few weeks later, my soul leaped with joy, for he expressed himself as being glad that I had given my heart to God, and even made a favorable expression concerning my decision to associate with the people of the church of God.

From this time I was much encouraged and determined to do what I could to help win my father and other loved ones to the Lord. I often read to him from the Bible and explained passages of Scripture as best I could, especially those that clearly taught a life of freedom from sin. Being a school-teacher, my work called me away from home much of the time, but the burden continued for the salvation of my father.

EFFORTS BY MAIL

A year after the Lord saved me, I went to a distant city to engage in the work of the Lord. One day I wrote a few words of exhortation to my father on the blank space of a little tract entitled Prepare for Heaven, and sent it with an earnest prayer that the Spirit of the Lord would apply the little message to my father's heart. In answer to this letter, he wrote me thus: "My Dear Daughter: I would give this whole world, were it mine to give, for this great salvation which you possess and are writing about." Then he opened his heart and frankly told me of his miserable condition and of how very hard it was for him to get right with God. He closed by asking me to pray God to send heavy conviction upon him.

It is needless to say that I became more earnest in praying and fasting for his soul. I felt much impressed to write him a helpful letter. Not only did I feel my inability to do so, but for lack of time deferred writing until I met with an accident that sprained my ankle badly, and then one day when I was unable to go about my work, I was reminded of my opportunity of writing to father. As I began writing and pouring out my heart to him, the blessings of the Lord rested upon me insomuch that it seemed I could write scarcely without effort; and as I mailed the letter, it was with an earnest prayer that the Lord would prepare my father for all that was written.

Some time later my father told me that he received this letter one morning before breakfast, and that although the letter was very lengthy, he sat down by the cook-stove and read it through. He said he marveled at it, for he had not believed that I was capable of writing the things that it contained. I do not remember what all I wrote, but I do praise God that the letter had the desired effect. Strange to say, though tobacco was not mentioned in the letter, yet when he had finished reading it, he thrust his hand into his pocket and seizing the thing that had almost become his constant companion, and holding it up before throwing it into the fire, said to my mother, with the tears streaming down his face, "I'll never touch it again if it kills me." Thank God, who had enabled him to make that determined decision. It meant much to him and was indeed a good beginning of his complete surrender to God. I had seen him try many times to quit using this thing that had so enslaved him. He had even gone as long as six months without it in his earnest efforts to break loose; but, sad to say, at the end of that time he had come to the end of his strength, and, not having God to help him, he was compelled, it seemed, to fully surrender again to the enemy and thus become more deeply enslaved. Now his decision was very definite, and in response to his earnest entreaties to the Lord, the abnormal appetite was removed.

The tone of his letter received a few days later indicated to me that he was under a weight of conviction and was ready and willing to humble his heart before the Lord. As there was soon to be a meeting, he said in his letter, "Daughter, will you please have those good brethren and sisters pray for me? The Bible tells us that the effectual fervent prayer of the righteous man availeth much." Portions of his letter were read to the congregation, and earnest, fervent prayer was offered in his behalf.

At the close of the meeting the minister and his wife accompanied me home for the purpose of imparting spiritual help to my father. Upon our arrival we found Father anxious to know the will of God, that he might find real rest to his soul, if possible. He listened attentively to the conversation and instruction, but it seemed that he was bound. He had a desire to pray, but said it seemed that he could not do so. He also said: "The Bible tells us that we shall know that we have passed from death unto life because we love the brethren, and now I must know it." We assured him that it was possible for him to have such knowledge, but that it must come through faith.

After spending much time in prayer and earnest efforts to help him, we had to let the case rest, and retired for the night heavily burdened for the deliverance of his soul. The next morning at breakfast I could see that my poor father was suffering, and his expression and pallor showed that he had spent a hard, restless night. Surely the Lord was granting the request made to me previously by letter, that he might have a deep conviction. His appetite being gone, he soon left the table.

THE SURRENDER

Arrangements had been made for him to take the minister and his wife to the city, a distance of fifteen miles, where they were to begin a series of meetings. He went to the barn to prepare for the trip, and while doing his chores, he started with a pitchfork of hay to the hack, but his heart was so heavy and the burden of sin so great that in the blackness of despair he cried out, "O Lord! if I drop into hell the next moment, let me go. I can't stand this any longer"; and, dropping his fork, he sank to the ground on his face pleading for help. The Friend that "sticketh closer than a brother" was right at his side. He heard that cry, for almost immediately my father was up rejoicing and laughing. "You are mocking God," was his first thought, and quite dumbfounded he dropped on his face again and tried to cry and plead as he had just been doing, but it was impossible. His heart was so light and the burden so completely gone that he could not remain prostrate longer.

Now, strange to say, this great change was all so simple and so sudden that the dear man could not comprehend at the time the glorious fact that he had just been "born again," had just "passed from death unto life." Still wondering over his changed condition, he finished his morning chores. He led two frisky colts out to water and afterward remarked how unusually well they behaved on this eventful morning. While they drank, he stood looking up into the heavens, then out upon the meadows and general surroundings. How beautiful everything appeared in the beginning of this new day! Suddenly there came into his heart such a love for the brethren that he wanted to rush into the house at once; but, having those colts, he had first to return to the barn. Then he came hastily to the house.

Instead of being so borne down and dejected, he came rushing through the front door laughing heartily. As he caught sight of me, the reality of the situation dawned upon him, and he rejoiced in this new-found life—real Bible salvation. He stretched out his arms to me over a rocker that stood between us and exclaimed as he embraced me, "O daughter, I believe!" Before he could say anything more on account of his great rejoicing, with a feeling of deep love and fellowship he reached one hand to Brother B. on the couch and the other to Sister B. in a rocker near the stove. Then he said, "Let us pray." As we knelt in real thanksgiving and praise, he began to pour out his heart in gratitude to God for salvation. Indeed, he was no longer bound by Satan but was free—yes, a new creature in Christ Jesus. When we arose rejoicing, even the unsaved members of the family felt the mighty power of God and gathered around weeping as we rejoiced and praised the Lord for this great victory.

MY OWN STRUGGLES AND VICTORIES

Now I wish to add just a few thoughts more in conclusion. All people do not receive this glorious experience in just the same way, or always manifest it as did my father. It was not my privilege at the time of my conversion to have the great flood of good feelings that he enjoyed; but instead I let my faith waver, and shortly after being saved I became seriously troubled with doubts and accusations. Just after my father had been rejoicing so happily, the devil almost crushed me with the thought that perhaps, after all, I had never been saved, as I had never realized such an experience as he had realized.

Could it be possible, I thought, that even though I have been so burdened for my father and have prayed so earnestly for him that I am not saved and never have been? The very thought almost made me faint-hearted. Then I remembered that the minister and others had confidence in me, and I knew that my life was completely changed, as I had really lost the desire for worldly pleasure, which I once so much enjoyed, and had become interested in the things of God. In reading my Bible, I saw that my life measured to its teachings so far as I understood. Therefore I took courage and tried to banish these accusations and leave my case with God.

But the enemy did not forget me, and it seemed that I should be drawn back into his whirlpool of doubts in spite of myself, more especially as I listened to my father in the next few weeks telling others about salvation. It was evident that he thought every one must obtain an experience of salvation in the same manner that he obtained it. My case was so different that finally I could suppress my feelings no longer, and boldly confessed to him one day that my experience was not like his and that if it ought to be I was not saved. Never shall I forget that moment. It meant so much to me. I wondered if he would lose confidence in my profession and if it was really true, and if it could possibly be true, that I was yet unsaved. These serious questionings were soon banished from my mind, for he looked at me and said, "Daughter, I know you are saved. Your life has proved it." Thank God, he did not doubt it; so I took courage and with a mighty effort put the accuser to flight again.

This experience was good for my father, as it had a tendency to balance him so that he would not be too exacting with others. Since that time other members of our family have sought God for the pardon of their sins, and with some of them the new life came in a calm, peaceful way, rather than with such emotional manifestations. The leadings of the Lord are wonderful, and the riches of his grace in the Christian life are inexhaustible.

My Spiritual Struggles and Victories

EXPERIENCE NUMBER 21

I was reared on one of the hilliest, stumpiest, and stoniest Canadian farms I have ever seen. How vividly there come to my mind my boyhood experiences of chopping cord-wood to pay my high-school expenses; of stumping, logging, and picking stones until the skin was worn off my fingers and the stones were stained with my blood. I then thought that mine was a very hard life, but I have long since looked back to those boyhood experiences as God's way of providing me with a physique that has enabled me to serve three years as a missionary in British North America, where the winds were intensely cold and where I was once for twenty-four hours lost in a blizzard at forty-five degrees below zero. In sharp contrast, I have been twenty-eight years in India's tropical heat. This was a preparation for my life-work and in my judgment is God's general method with all his people.

When I was a boy of ten summers, a boyhood friend of my father's visited him. They were taking a walk, and, unnoticed, I followed them. Then I overheard my father's friend praise my brothers and sisters, but say of me, "Frank will never amount to much." My father vigorously protested and sang my praises until I made this resolution: "I must not disappoint my father. I will do something worthy of consideration." That hour I was intellectually awakened.

Parents, let your young people know that you believe in them. About the same time our pastor preached a missionary sermon, at the end of which he circulated a subscription. When the paper came to me, I said to my father, "May I subscribe?" He replied, "If you earn and pay your own money, you may." I subscribed one dollar. I had it earned long before the collectors came around, and wished either that I had subscribed more or that the collectors might come soon. That subscription was the beginning which ended in my giving myself. Parents, give your children a chance to link themselves definitely with Jesus in saving a lost world.

MY CONVERSION

When I was a boy of about thirteen, my father said to me one evening at the setting of the sun, "Water the stock." Soon some boys arrived, and, being a real boy, I forgot my work and played.

A little later my father asked, "Have you done what I told you?"

"Yes, father," I replied.

He knew I had not, and I even now recall that he said not a word but walked away in the twilight so burdened and bowed because of hearing a falsehood from his own boy that it suddenly gave him the appearance of an old man. The boys left, and I watered the stock. Then, boy like, I forgot, went to bed and slept. During the next forenoon Mother called me to her and said:

"Do you know your father neither went to bed nor slept all last night?"

I replied, "No, Mother, I do not know. Why didn't he sleep?"

Mother's answer was, "Your father spent all last night praying for you."

My saintly mother's words and tears went through my heart like an arrow and rang like a bell in my ears, and I became powerfully convicted of sin. Just following that a series of revival meetings were held which continued for several weeks. I became a seeker and had no rest until I found it in penitence and a consciousness of pardoned sin. I was the only convert during the meetings, and critics said, "He will backslide in a few weeks. The revival is a failure." But I am here to tell the story that I am still saved by grace.

I could never reward my father for that night of prevailing prayer, but he lived to see me become a minister, a missionary, and to hold the highest position on the mission field, and then the Lord called him to his eternal reward. My mother entered into rest about two years previous to that time.

It is my hope and prayer that the story of my father's night of prevailing prayer may encourage other parents to pray as he did. Parents may not always through prayer be able to break the wills of their children and compel them to surrender to Jesus, but I do believe that my father prayed until God sent such conviction through the Holy Spirit that sin became such an unbearable burden that I gladly yielded my will to the will of my God; prayed until my sins were pardoned, the burden removed, and I was genuinely converted. I firmly believe that the same heavenly Father will hear the cry of other parents, and for their encouragement I leave this testimony concerning God's answer to my father's fervent prayers.

After my conversion I rejoiced many days in the delight of that precious experience. For months I had a real and precious joy in the consciousness of pardoned sin, but after a time I found that I did not have a continuous, abiding peace and rest. There was a longing for something more than it seemed I now possessed. As a boy I tried very hard to be good, and as I look back I believe that I lived a very correct outward life. I lived among a very godly people, who set a high ideal before me, one to which I felt I could not live. I observed my daily prayers, but suffered many an inward defeat.

MY SPIRITUAL STRUGGLES

I can not now recall that I ever heard a sermon on heart-purity or victory over the power of sin. No person in the congregation where our family attended meetings professed holiness, nor do I remember that the experience was talked about. The people did speak of "having religion" and "more religion." There were people in the congregation whom I still believe lived holy lives, and the testimony of their lives convicted me, for I knew that they had an abiding joy and peace in their religion that I had not. I therefore became very much dissatisfied with my inner life and was struggling all the time for an experience such as I knew others enjoyed.

The weekly testimony of a man who attended our prayer-meetings was, "I have just enough religion to make me miserable." That is, he had too much religion to get his pleasure out of the world and not enough to get it out of his religion. I always felt that that man told the experience I then had. For three years I endured that exceedingly unsatisfactory religious experience. I then attended a revival and went forward for prayer night after night, but no relief came to my poor burdened heart. As my case became more desperate, I recalled the story of Jacob. He prayed until the morning, and at the rising of the sun the angel appeared and blessed him. I spent several nights in prayer, but found no relief.

GAINING THE VICTORY

On Saturday morning about sunrise I was on a straw stack in the barnyard with a long hay-knife cutting across the stack to loosen the straw to feed the cattle. While thus working and in a despondent, meditative mood, wondering what I could do, there seemed suddenly to float out before me in the air in illuminated letters, "John three sixteen." I began to read, "God so loved the world." I reasoned then that God so loved me that "he gave his only begotten Son." All was clear thus far. Then I came to that all-inclusive word, "whosoever." I stopped at "whosoever" and recalled the story I heard of Richard Baxter, who said, "I would rather have the word 'whosoever' in John three sixteen than have Richard Baxter, for then I should at once be tempted to believe it was for some other Richard Baxter."

I reasoned, "I know that my name is in that 'whosoever.'" I then read on—"believeth on him." "Do I believe on him?" This was the next question to be settled. During several years I had, in competition for a Sunday-school prize, recited the whole four Gospels. In thought I ran over what the New Testament said about Jesus and cried out, "I believe every word of the gospel; Lord, I do believe."

Then I read on—"should not perish." Quick as a flash I saw the weak place in my faith. I had been believing on Jesus, but feeling that I should perish. At that point I sprang to my feet on the straw stack and read it over again—"Should not perish, but have everlasting life." Then I saw that through doubt I had treated the promise as though it read "should perish and not have everlasting life." I cried out, "Lord, I will reverse it no longer. I will believe it as it reads."

Then I seemed to have another inspiration. I had long been troubled about understanding what it meant to believe. I had worked out a theory that if I could for a moment forget everything else in the world and see Jesus on the cross, that would be "exercising saving faith"; and when praying, I would find myself trying to do that. I now asked myself this question: "How do you believe your mother's promise?" The answer was at once, "I believe because I believe in my mother, the promiser." The next moment I realized that believing Mother's promises was not a mental effort and struggle such as I had been going through for years, but a mental rest. I just believed that her promise was true without any effort whatever, not because I felt it, but because Mother made it. Then I cried, "Jesus made this promise, and I believe it."

Then I waited and looked again into my heart for the feeling, but no feeling came. I then saw clearly for the first time that I was trusting partly in Jesus and partly to my feelings. Presently the Spirit showed me that feeling never saves any one, that only Jesus saves. I remember that, standing on the straw stack, I cried out, "O Jesus! I put my all on thy promise, and I will leave all with thee." But alas! again I waited for the feeling as a witness, and was sure it would come, but it did not come. I was still trusting partly in Christ and partly to feeling. At last I turned away from looking for feeling and cried aloud: "My Jesus, I stake my all on John three sixteen. If I never have any feeling and if I am lost, I will quote this promise before thee at the judgment and say, 'I cast my little all upon it and trusted it, but it failed me. It is not my fault; it is thine.'"

I had finally, after years of struggling, come where I trusted wholly "in the word of the Lord." Then suddenly I received a definite assurance and great heart-warming peace and joy.

At last the witness of the Spirit was mine. Leaping from the straw stack, I ran to my mother, threw my arms around her neck, and shouted, "Mother, I am fully saved! I am fully saved!"

Up to that time I had not had any teaching concerning an experience of sanctification or holiness and had heard no testimonies concerning such an experience, except the testimony of the life of Christians who were living it and professing it under another name. There was in the congregation where I worshiped a sweet-faced, white-haired saint whom we called Mother Robinson. She had prayed a drunkard husband into the kingdom, and my memory even to this day recalls her high type of Christian experience, and I want to bear my strongest possible testimony to the power there is in the testimony of a pure, sweet, and kind life.

Now after years of study and hearing the testimony of many, it is clear to me that during those years as a boy I prayed myself through to the abiding life and what I now believe to be the experience of Scriptural holiness, which, as I understand it, is such a freedom from sin, self-will, and selfishness, and such a passionate love for Jesus, that the heart longs above all things for his approval, companionship, guidance, and blessing, and that gratefully and joyfully gives Jesus "in all things the preeminence."

Thought He Had Sinned Away His Day of Grace

EXPERIENCE NUMBER 22

The enemy of souls has laid many plans and has many devices to deceive people and harass their minds and thereby cause them to bring unnecessarily heavy burdens upon themselves. One of his common impositions is to make a person think that he has committed the unpardonable sin and that all hope of ever obtaining favor with God again is forever gone. When such persons are told that they are laboring under a delusion, and that there is hope for them; that others have felt the same way and formed the same conclusion, but afterwards learned that it was only a deception of the enemy, and were able to renounce the delusion and obtain a good experience and keep it, the answer in most cases is, "My case is different." "Had I taken advantage of past opportunities when I had a chance to do so, I might have been saved, but now it is too late."

Time after time I have labored with those who were sure that their cases were "different" from that of any one else, and that hope was beyond their reach. The situation and feelings seemed so real that no amount of reasoning or evidence to the contrary could change their minds until they became submissive enough to submit themselves to the mercy of God and accept advice and counsel and act upon it. Then they were very soon liberated from the oppressions of the enemy and set free by the grace of God.

One laboring under a deception frequently undergoes as deep suffering of mind and soul as if the situation and conditions were real. A lady once received what was supposed to be an authentic report that her son had been killed in a railway wreck. Circumstances were such that she could receive no communication from him, which apparently added evidence to the truthfulness of the story. Her mother-heart was grief-stricken. In the anguish of her bereavement she refused to be comforted. Later she was told that there was a possibility of his having escaped death, that he was probably yet alive, and that evidence had been received to that effect. No, her feelings were too real, her grief was too great, for her to be deceived, she declared. One day her son arrived home sound and well, and did not even know that there had been a train-wreck at the place whence the report came. The mother then found that her sorrow and grief had been groundless. She accepted the status of affairs, cast aside the false report and her bad feelings, and was happy.

Not long ago I met an old acquaintance, a man above seventy years of age, whom I had not seen for many years. At the time of our former meeting he was enjoying the blessings of a Christian experience and was happy in the service of the Lord. Through devotional neglect, and perhaps for other reasons, he began to entertain doubts concerning his spiritual experience, and he questioned whether or not he had any right, under the circumstances, to lay claim to Christian fellowship with those whom he knew to be spiritual. He knew of nothing sinful that he had done, and he needed not to waver in faith. But the tempter was there to suggest that he had lost his experience and might just as well give up the struggle. He then concluded that the brethren did not have confidence in him, and therefore he dropped his profession.

His heart was still tender, and he did not feel disposed to indulge in sin. In a short time he made "another start" to serve the Lord and tried to repent; but, having so little to repent over, and finding it difficult to have the same earnestness as before, he claimed the victory "by faith," but was soon in "doubting castle" again. These up-and-down experiences continued for many months, during which his spiritual realm was more down than up. Discouragement laid hold upon him, despair followed hard on his track, and the enemy whispered that it was of no use to try any more. The way began to be more and more dreary. Occasionally, however, he was seized with a feeling of desperation to break loose from the state of lethargy into which he had fallen, but alas! his victories were of short duration. These experiences were followed by the accusations of the enemy that he was possessed with devils. Brethren who prayed with him declared that such was not the case.

The darkest scriptures of judgment and everlasting destruction seemed to have been written for him, and, as he viewed the matter, they exactly fitted his case. He had doubted so often when it seemed the Lord was offering a helping hand, that now it was too late; the last cord was severed, the last ray of hope had vanished. It was no difficult matter to believe that he had committed the unpardonable sin, and that God had forever hid his face from him. He resigned himself to the hopelessness of the situation, to meet his fate at the end of his life here upon earth and spend eternity in the regions of the lost. He spent a number of years in this condition.

At the time of our recent visit in a private home, I felt much concerned about his deliverance from such a state and condition. Upon my approaching him on the subject, he immediately informed me that it was useless to waste any of my efforts on him, for his was a hopeless case, as he had sinned against the Holy Ghost. Having met similar cases before, I assured him that there was hope for him, and told him that I could prove by the Word of God and by his own testimony that he had not committed the crime that would cause him to be forever lost, as he had supposed.

Taking my Bible, I turned to Heb. 10:29, which reads as follows: "Of how much sorer punishment, suppose ye, shall he be thought worthy, who hath trodden under foot the Son of God, and hath counted the blood of the covenant, wherewith he was sanctified, an unholy thing, and hath done despite unto the Spirit of grace?"

"Have you trodden under foot the Son of God as herein mentioned?" he was then asked. "No," he replied; "I have never doubted that there is a God nor that Jesus Christ is his Son."

"Have you counted the 'blood of the covenant an unholy thing,' that is, that there is no more virtue in the blood of Jesus Christ than there is in the blood of a cow or some other unholy thing?"

"No, sir. I have never denied the power of the blood of Jesus nor 'done despite to the Spirit of grace,'" he replied.

"Then, according to the Bible and your own testimony, you have not blasphemed against the Holy Ghost, nor, as you say, committed the unpardonable sin by sinning against the Holy Ghost. You must forever cease to entertain the idea that you have committed such a sin."

He reluctantly admitted the truth in regard to that point, but said, "There is such a thing as a man's going too far, of trifling so with God that the Spirit of God will no longer strive with him." It was clearly pointed out to him that he had never reached such an experience and that he should cast aside his doubts and fears and call upon God, and was assured that the Lord would save him. He then declared that he had no will of his own, no power to exercise his will if he had any, and was helpless. I told him that any one who could read human nature would at once conclude that he was a man of strong will-power, and that no doubt he frequently made others aware of that fact. His wife said, "That is true; he knows very well how to exercise his will-power."

He was then told to assert his manhood and take a decided stand, to which he replied:

"I have no manhood; I have no power to assert myself in any way."

"But," I replied, "you have been in this town for the past few days, and have asserted your manhood during your entire visit by acting the part of a perfect gentleman. What you need to do now is to kneel with us here in prayer and yield yourself to God, and he will save you the same as he has saved others who thought they were beyond the reach of mercy."

"But my case is different; my heart is hardened like stone; I can not pray; I have no feeling."

"Almost every one in your condition thinks his case is different. If you act according to the instructions given, you will soon be different. Your heart will be changed. Do your part in making the effort, and the Lord will help you to pray, and you will have all the feeling necessary."

We knelt in prayer, laid our hands upon his head, and with a fervent prayer rebuked the deceptive and binding power of Satan, and asked the Lord to save him. He made an effort to pray, but his few words were soon mingled with his sobs and feelings of deepest contrition. A few minutes later he arose praising God for salvation. His doubts and fears had vanished, and his burden was gone. He was once more a free man and had no more fears of death and the judgment. The next day he returned home with a joyful heart. I have frequently heard from him since that time, and he has always sent a message concerning his victorious life.

There are many others who have been harassed by the enemy in like manner; who have lost all hope of recovering their favor with God; who think that they are "different," "hard-hearted," "hopeless," "have sinned away the day of grace," "are under the control of Satan," or in some such like condition. Yet God in his love is extending mercy and only waiting for them to discard their deceptive ideas and accept his grace.

Spiritual Tests

EXPERIENCE NUMBER 23

It is not always concerning temporal things and business affairs and such like that we are tested. But it is the business of the enemy of souls to contest every step on the way to victory. He will contest our salvation and, if possible, get a person to reason with him; and when you reason with the devil, you find him a good reasoner, if you allow him to follow his own line of thought. He will quote Scripture, and give plausible illustrations and logical reasonings. But when he is met as Christ met him, with a "Thus saith the Lord," "It is written," and then told what is written and where it is written, and such like, he is not very long in taking his departure. But just begin to reason, and he will entangle you in argument until you find yourself badly perplexed, unless, like the Master, you give him a sharp rebuke and command him to take his departure.

Perhaps it would be a benefit to some one for me to give a little of my own personal experience in this respect. At the age of fifteen I was converted, receiving a real change of heart. The enemy of my soul was never able to deny that fact, neither did he undertake it. For about ten years I lived to what light I had, and after that began to obtain more light in regard to entering into a deeper experience of divine life, or entire sanctification. I was away from home and had no one to teach me the way of holiness, but the Lord began to instruct me in his Word, and after a few months I was enabled to see just what the Lord required of me in order to obtain the experience desired.

I had felt a hungering and thirsting for something more, for a deeper experience. I had been taught, however, that this satisfying experience could not be obtained until just before the time of death; but as I read in the Word that without holiness no man should see the Lord (Heb. 12:14), that we were to live in righteousness and holiness all the days of our life (Luke 1:75), and that Jesus in his last prayer (John 17:17-20) prayed that we might have that experience, I began to see very clearly what my privilege was. His Word told me, "As he is, so are we in this world," and, "We ought to walk even as he walked"; and this was a closer walk with God than I had been accustomed to enjoy.

It was not long until I reached the point where I made a full consecration, and died the death to the world, and then, like the apostles for whom Jesus prayed, I was in the world, but not of the world, having had that worldly disposition taken out of my heart. When I reached the point where I positively knew that everything was laid upon the altar Christ Jesus, then I realized of a truth that the altar sanctified the gift, and my heart was cleansed from all unrighteousness. The Bible began to open up to me as a new book, and as I went about my Master's business, doing his will as far as he made it known, I had many rich experiences. Although, being of a very quiet disposition naturally, I could not leap and shout as some, yet it was my privilege to be filled with all the fulness of God.

A few months later I was called by the Lord to accept a responsible position in his work. For some months everything went so smoothly that I had perfect victory all the way along and nothing that I could call a severe trial or battle, because my eyes were stayed upon the Lord. But there came a time for advancing further against the enemy, and the Lord saw it was necessary for me to know more about a perfect faith and trust in him in order to deal with other souls. So he permitted me to be tested, to fit me for the work he had for me to do.

Although my soul had been abounding in the riches of his glory for these months as I was busily engaged in my work, one day a suggestion was made to me by a silent voice that I had not had any overflowing blessings for a few days. This did not disturb me, for I felt at perfect peace with God. But soon the same suggestion was presented again and again. Finally the silent voice or impression came on this wise: "Now you have been in this condition almost a week." I felt that my soul during that time had been at peace with God, and I was trusting my case in his hands. I began, however, to search my consecration, as the accuser suggested that there must surely be something wrong.

I began to search my heart, and said, "If there is anything wrong, Lord, I will make it all right," and I asked the Lord to search me. Feeling that all was fully in the hands of the Lord, I was about to dismiss the matter from my mind; but this suggestion came: "If you were sanctified, you would not have a lack of that great joy." Then I said, "Lord, if I am not sanctified, I am willing to get sanctified." So I began to reconsecrate myself to the Lord, and presently I realized that I was fully consecrated to God. Again I was ready to dismiss the matter, but the voice said, "When a person falls from sanctification, he loses his justification also, because he must commit sin in order to fall." Yes, I realized that was so, and then came the words, "You are not saved." I saw at once that it was the enemy, instead of the Lord, talking to me, and like a flash from heaven I rebuked him. I said, "I know I am saved through the grace of God; yes, and sanctified, too." And I boldly declared it, whereupon the enemy took his departure. He saw that he was the one defeated, instead of me.

The enemy had thought that because I was young in the Lord's work I was unable to know his devices. But the Lord was a match for him, and lifted up a standard against him, instead of allowing me to be defeated and overthrown. The Lord knew just how far to permit me to be tried and tempted. This experience has been a source of much help to me since that time; not only for myself, but in dealing with others. The devil is sure to overstep the mark, and we can have the victory over him as long as we keep our eyes stayed upon the Lord. And we can say like Paul, "I can do all things through Christ, which strengtheneth me."

There are some who worry and fret and have an abundance of trouble when it is their own fault; and if they would put forth as great an effort to gain a victory and keep it as they do to pet their troubles, there would be a wonderful change and the enemy of souls would be defeated.

A few years ago I met a brother who was weighted down with trouble and sorrows much more than with the glory of God, and was much of the time mourning over his trials and temptations, until his lot did really seem to be a sad one. During my Christian experience I had been having sweeping victory over the powers of the enemy, even through the severe trials and temptations, because I had kept my eyes upon the Lord, and had looked for victories instead of trials. In considering the case of the brother, although I was young in the gospel work, I concluded that if people were in such a condition it was their own fault, and that I could feel as bad as any one if I desired. So I concluded to experiment, but first asked the Lord not to permit me to fall into the hands of the devil.

Accordingly, though I had nothing whatever to feel bad about, I threw myself on a couch and began to sigh and try to feel bad over something. It was but a few minutes until I really did begin to feel miserable. Some one came and desired to know if I was in trouble, but I turned away and would not answer. In a short time I was feeling miserable enough to weep and moan, and even bewail my condition. I then went to my room, fastened the door, and began to call mightily upon God for deliverance from such a condition. I had to put forth no little effort and take God at his word and gain the victory over the powers of Satan. I there learned the lesson that any one can feel bad and have a sorrowful time whether or not he really has anything to feel bad about; but I never desired to repeat the experiment. I have also found that God has power not only to deliver from such a condition, but to keep the soul filled with glory even through the severest testings.

The Confession of a Murderer

EXPERIENCE NUMBER 24

While traveling in evangelistic and missionary work a few years ago another minister and I met with a congregation in a Western city. When I entered the place of worship, my eyes fell upon a woman sitting near the altar. She was an object of pity because of her affliction, which was of a very peculiar nature and noticeable at a glance. Although she was a stranger to me and began uttering such expressions as "Praise the Lord!" and "Halleluiah!" yet I felt that I discerned a false spirit and was strongly impressed that she was possessed with a murderous and deceptive spirit. At the close of the service we were asked to pray for her healing. It was evident that she received no help, and although she made a loud profession of religion, my conviction was deepened that my former impressions were correct, and furthermore that she was guilty of murdering an unborn child.

After the next service this woman and her husband invited me to their home. I went with a prayer that God would send conviction upon them and save them from their deception and lost condition. After spending some time in social conversation, I began to talk with them about their spiritual condition. At first there was some resentment; for the enemy of souls had made them believe that it was no great crime, in fact, no crime at all; that she was really justified in committing the deed; that as no one else knew of it and was not likely to know, she could cover her sin and go on with a profession as a Christian and receive the fellowship of other Christian people. She was kindly told that she had a false spirit, one foreign to the Spirit of God.

She broke down and, with tears streaming down her cheeks, confessed that she had destroyed her unborn child, and said that the affliction soon fastened upon her as leprosy did upon Miriam. Not until the time of our visit did she fully realize the heinousness of her sin nor feel the weight of her guilt. By justifying herself in the act and professing religion without repentance, she had opened the door of her heart to deception.

But now as she became awakened to her real condition, the enemy whispered, as he has done to many others under similar circumstances: "It is too late now; there is no hope; for 'they which do such things shall not inherit the kingdom of God'" (Gal. 5:21). She was told that those who do such things and cover their sins or continue to do them without forsaking them and without repenting are the ones who will not inherit the kingdom of God. "He that covereth his sins shall not prosper; but whoso confesseth and forsaketh them shall have mercy" (Prov. 28:13).

Prayer was offered in her behalf, the evil spirits were rebuked, and she realized a gleam of hope for her deliverance, not only from the deception into which she had fallen, but also from her sin. She began to realize that God was ready to forgive her and set her burdened, repentant heart free, and accept her as his child. Oh, how unworthy she felt!

Now came the question, "Must I confess this deed to the church, to my neighbors, and to the world?" "No, the sin you committed was against yourself and against God," I answered, "and it will do the church and the world no good to know of it. In fact, a knowledge of it might be an injury to some weaker ones. You have confessed it to God and he has forgiven you, and as no one else is injured, there is no one else to whom it need be confessed."

When she had been made free from her guilt by the grace of God, she could then come to him with faith for the healing of her body, and she was delivered from her affliction.

Another case was that of a gambler in one of the Western States who had often been warned against the evils of gambling, but who would not heed the admonitions of friends. He continued his life of folly until the time came when, in the midst of his revelry, a contention arose between him and a fellow gambler. The provocation was so great that both drew deadly weapons, and to save his own life and at the same time to wreak vengeance upon the other man, he fired the fatal shot, and his antagonist fell dead at his feet.

Immediately sorrow filled his heart because he had shed human blood, thus making himself a murderer. In a short time he was behind prison-bars to await trial, and the following message was flashed over the wires to his brother: "I am in trouble; killed a man today; come." Brothers, parents, and friends came with their sympathy and tears, money and influence. Court after court convened, and from year to year the case was continued or sentence was rendered and suspended. For a long time he was under sentence of death. Money and influence prolonged the case, and the indications were that it might be deferred many more years if sufficient money was available.

It was while in that dungeon awaiting the fulfilment of the death-sentence that he felt the wooings of the Spirit of the Lord. He read the New Testament and wrote to us to pray for him. He finally confessed his sins to the Lord and found peace to his soul. He then began to appropriate the promises to his own case for deliverance from prison. God honored his faith and the faith of His servants who were offering earnest prayers that he might be delivered. Contrary to the advice of relatives and friends, he dismissed all legal counsel and decided to place his case entirely in the hands of the God of heaven, who delivered Daniel out of the lions' den and Peter out of prison. In a short time his faith was rewarded by a message being flashed over the wires for the authorities to open the prison-doors and let him go free. Since then he has spent much time visiting prisoners and encouraging them to put their trust in the Lord, who is mighty to save.

Making a Complete Surrender

EXPERIENCE NUMBER 25

From the time of my conversion in early life I longed to be useful in helping others to find the way of salvation. But my inability and lack of talent was an apparent barrier, and caused me to almost despair of ever being able to accomplish the desire of my heart.

Though I felt that I was a Christian, yet I had a longing in my soul for a closer walk with God. There were times when I had spiritual struggles within and without, and I did not know how to be an "overcomer," as mentioned in the Bible.

A few years later, while living in Ohio, I was awakened to the fact that the Lord had promised the gift of the Holy Spirit to his believing children and that it was my privilege to obtain that experience wherein I could enjoy that "great grace" which was upon them all who were assembled at one place after Pentecost. My heart yearned for the experience that the people of those apostolic days enjoyed; and as I read about how willing the Lord was to "give the Holy Ghost to them that believe," and read that we were promised the "Comforter," who would abide in our hearts, I decided to have the experience.

My religious instructors gave me no encouragement; for they had not attained to such an experience themselves and did not think it attainable in this life. But undaunted, and determined to have relief for my burdened soul, I sought the Lord earnestly to reveal to me the secret of obtaining that abundant grace which I was convinced was within my reach if I could only learn how to obtain it.

The time came when my prayers were answered, and I was enabled to make a complete consecration to the will of God. But before reaching that point, I many times fell upon my knees or prostrated myself before the Lord in earnest supplication for that grace. In the meantime I met others who had received it, and I realized more than ever that what they possessed was just the thing for which I had been seeking. There were yet two points that seemed to hinder me in my final efforts. My desire was to have such an outpouring of the Spirit as would cause me to leap and shout the same as some others did when they received the Holy Spirit. The second was that there was one thing which I had not fully yielded to the will of God. Regarding that thing I made a conditional surrender—that if God would give me the experience and then show me that I held a wrong attitude, I would then yield the point. I thought the Lord ought to accept my consecration and give me the experience I had so long sought. But he would not do so.

I began to submit myself to the Lord more fully, and he more clearly opened my understanding to his Word and more definitely shed rays of light upon my pathway concerning the point in question; then came the words of Jesus, "Walk in the light while ye have the light, lest ye go into darkness." My duty was now as clear to me as the morning sun. There was no rebellion in my heart, the surrender was complete, and I could with confidence say that my consecration reached the will of God on every point, regarding all the things I could call to my mind and also everything that might present itself in the future. There was no doubt concerning my having made what we sometimes call a Bible consecration.

Then I realized that I had a right to claim the promise and receive its fulfilment. As I did so, laying claim to the promise as mine and declaring the work was done because the Word of God said so, that whatever touched the altar was made holy, I knew that by faith I had touched the altar, Jesus Christ, and was made holy. I had become willing to receive the blessing in any way that the Lord saw fit to bestow it. Just at the time that I claimed the blessing as mine, quietness reigned. It did not cause me to leap and shout as I had been expecting, but in a quiet manner the Holy Spirit witnessed the work wrought in my soul. I learned that the grace and glory or spiritual power that one possesses is not dependent upon outward demonstrations of the body. While one may leap and shout, another person of a different temperament may remain quiet and yet be drinking just as deeply from the fountain of life.

Although many years have passed, yet I have never once doubted the work wrought in my soul at that time. Amidst the deepest trials of life, sorrow, sickness, and adversity, I have found a sweet solace by trusting all away with Him who understands our every need.

Dark days and shadows of life may come, trials and temptations may present themselves on every hand, the soul may be weighted down with burdens that are heavy to bear, and accusations of the enemy and hours of severe testing may come like a flood; yet for the trusting soul the Spirit of the Lord will lift up a standard against the enemy and lead onward to victory. To me the Lord has been "a very present help in trouble" and a friend in time of need.

When I see others struggling along and yearning for that experience wherein their souls can be satisfied, my wishes are that they make an unconditional surrender, know without a doubt that their consecration is complete and that they are in all points consecrated to the will of God. It is then that the promise can be claimed and the fulfilment realized.

The greatest sinner on the face of the earth can find pardon through the atonement of Jesus Christ by forsaking his sins, confessing them to the Lord, and believing on him for deliverance. In like manner every believer can be filled with the Holy Spirit and abound in the riches of the grace of God.

Interesting Narratives and Helpful Instruction

Success and happiness in the Christian life do not always depend upon favorable surroundings; under the most adverse and trying circumstances men and women have made the greatest strides in spiritual advancement and power. There may be occasional sorrows and suffering along the way, but shall these things cast a gloom over our lives, even though at times they be prolonged and severe? By no means should we allow opposition, persecution, sorrow, suffering, mistakes, blunders, failures, and such like to cause defeat and a giving way to discouragement. The discouraged person is "no good," no matter where you find him. We must rise in the midst of our trials and in the name and strength of the Lord shake off discouragements.

Trials will come, but what of it? Others have had just as severe trials, and have surmounted them, and you and I can do the same. There will be times when oppressions will be

felt that seem grievous to bear; when even the humble
followers of Christ will feel that the lines of
communication between them and the Lord have been
severed; when prayers will seem to fall to the earth and the
heavens seem as brass, and the burdened soul will cry out
for help when there seems to be no help. At such times
there needs to be a patient waiting upon the Lord, heart-
searching, and humble submission to his will. Under such
circumstances it is well to heed the advice of the Psalmist:
"Wait patiently upon the Lord, and he shall bring it to
pass." Then is the time to trust and not be afraid.

It was at such a time that Jesus felt that his burden was
more than he could bear and asked that, if possible, the cup
of suffering be removed, that he might not have to pass
through the severe ordeal that was facing him. His
humanity weakened and shuddered at the approach of the
greatest trial of his life. But he humbly submitted and said,
"Father, not my will, but thy will, be done." It was then that
angels came and ministered unto him; the gates of glory
were thrown open, the burden was gone, and he could go
forth as a captive set free.

As he left that place of prayer, that place of victory, it was
to face the foe in the hottest of the fight. Although he was
upheld by the unseen presence of the Father and
strengthened by the angels, nevertheless in the darkest hour
of the conflict he cried out, "My God, my God, why hast
thou forsaken me?" But even in this final test he said,
"Father, into thy hands I commend my Spirit." This was
followed by the unprecedented glories of the resurrection.
What a wonderful lesson to us of submission and trust!

FAILED TO FORGIVE THOSE WHO HAD WRONGED HIM

An unforgiving disposition will hinder one from being humble or from reaching the necessary point of submission. When Stephen was being stoned by his persecutors, his dying prayer was, "Lord, lay not this sin to their charge." One Sunday when I was conducting an inquiry-service in a State prison, after I had commented on these words of Jesus, "If ye forgive not men their trespasses, neither will your Father forgive your trespasses," a prisoner arose and said, "For years I have sought the Lord, but never before have I known what hindered me from obtaining peace to my soul. But now I see it is because I have held a grudge against those who have wronged me. I forgive them." Peace came into his soul as he yielded this point.

DESPONDENCY AND DISCOURAGEMENT

Instead of counting your trials and indulging in dark forebodings, throw away such feelings by counting your past blessings if you can think of no present blessings. When Paul and Silas were in prison with their feet fastened in the stocks, the pain in their lacerated backs no doubt often reminded them of the cruel treatment they had received at the hands of their enemies; but they looked away from their trials, and, "counting all things joy," at the midnight hour they were rejoicing, singing songs, and praising God. The result was marvelous. Had they set themselves to complaining, they would have spent a miserable night.

A sister was once just at the point of throwing down her shield of faith and ceasing her efforts in serving the Lord, because of some difficulty which had arisen between her husband and one of the brethren, and in which in a sense she also was involved. She had always entertained implicit confidence in the brother, but now said she could never have confidence in him again. Had it been some worldly person, she could have overlooked the matter, but to have one of the brethren make such statements was more than she could endure. However, she relented, and before she could gain the necessary victory, she had to make a decision to stand true to God regardless of the source of the trial.

At this point is where many fail, not because the trial is greater than some other through which they have passed, but because it comes from an entirely unexpected source.

UNNECESSARY SELF-ACCUSATIONS

A woman and her husband who were ministers were once drawn into a difficulty with others and had to call for aid in making an adjustment. When the time came for a consideration of the matter, she humbly and nobly did her part, to the satisfaction of all concerned. Although there was nothing demoralizing about the case, yet she felt very humiliated to think that she, a minister, should have thus become involved in such a contention, and thought that the brother who was called to help in the adjustment would never have confidence in her again. For four years she worried over the matter, often losing sleep at night, and felt herself gradually weakening in spirituality and courage.

One day she met the brother, and he expressed himself as having had implicit confidence in her during the entire period of the four years. Immediately she took courage, but she had needlessly undergone untold sufferings through accusations that were all imaginary. Worrying does no one any good. It is useless to worry before a thing happens, much less after it happens. Most people worry over imaginary things, over things that never have nor never will come to pass.

A sister who had lived a godly life and had prayed for her family for years, became much troubled because none of them would become Christians. She began to accuse herself of not being right in the sight of God, but she was reminded that even Jesus himself, although he was the Son of God, was not able to have all his kinsmen and townsmen to follow him. She then learned to leave the responsibility with her family and the Lord after she had done all she could, realizing that her soul was clear.

TROUBLED ABOUT MAKING CONFESSIONS

One woman was troubled over her past life, feeling that she should make a public confession, which would endanger the lives of others. She said it seemed that God was far away from her. Upon investigation it was learned that her trouble was of such a nature that it would do her or nobody else any good to make such a confession, but was a matter that could be settled only between herself and God. Not until she learned this could she have peace of mind and reach the place where she could find deliverance.

An actress was married to a respectable young man in Ohio. Their home was an ideal one in the country. Three children graced their domestic circle, and there was apparently nothing to mar the happiness of their Christian home. One day the wife and eldest daughter went to visit the pastor who had for years been their spiritual advisor. He expressed his congratulations to her for her attainments in life, pleasant surroundings, and the extraordinary abilities of her children.

Just before leaving the house of the pastor, she requested a private interview with him. When alone with him she said: "Judging from outward appearances, you have believed me to be a very happy woman. But for many years my heart has been sad, and I have constantly carried a heavy burden. Sometimes it seemed to be more than I could bear. Before my marriage I was allured into sin of a disgraceful nature, but my husband believed me to have always maintained an irreproachable character, and I have never told him otherwise. Since our marriage I have always been true to him. Many times during these years I have been just at the point of unburdening my heart by revealing to him this secret and placing myself at his mercy; but somehow I have always been checked or prevented from doing so. I have carried the heavy burden until I can carry it no longer. Please tell me what to do."

The wise old pastor, with deep feelings of compassion, said: "Good woman, you have carried an unnecessary burden all these years. Your husband knew nothing of your sin; it will do him no good to know of it now, but, on the other hand, a knowledge of it might bring an unnecessary burden upon him, and cause his implicit confidence to give place to suspicion. Why should you thus bring feelings of reproach upon yourself and family? They are a thousand times better off without a knowledge of it. Go bury it in oblivion; cast it from your mind forever. God has forgiven you long ago. Such matters are to be settled between you and him alone; go and sin no more." She obeyed and went forth a happy woman. Her burden was gone.

If all spiritual advisors were as wise as this pastor in giving instruction to those in need of help, much suffering would be averted. There are thousands of people today carrying heavy burdens that God has not placed upon them, but has long ago forgiven because of their repentance. Such persons have allowed the enemy of their souls to unnecessarily burden them with accusations and false impressions. These they should have cast aside, declaring their freedom in the name of Jesus.

ACCUSED GOD OF NOT BEING JUST

There are others who accuse God of not being just, or blame him for not answering their prayers, when the fact is, their lives have not been such as would give them an assurance that God would answer their prayers. A young sister who had for some time been drifting into worldliness was called to the bedside of her dying father. She was much concerned about him and asked a special favor of the Lord concerning him, and because her request was not granted in just the manner requested, she permitted her mind to be filled with doubts and infidelity. She blamed God for not answering, and then she began to have struggles with hardness of heart, which she had never known before. This caused her to become alarmed, and she sought the counsel of a minister. He cited her to 1 John 3:22—"And whatsoever we ask we receive of him, because we keep his commandments, and do those things that are pleasing in his sight." She acknowledged that she had not been living right, and therefore had no right to blame God for not answering her prayers.

WHEN THE TEMPTER COMES OFTENEST

The tempter comes oftenest where the temptation has not been completely put away and where there is lack of decision against it. Many people are like the drunkard. He desires to cease drinking, but says, "Just one more drink; then I am done." When that has been taken he says, "One more, only one; then I am forever done with strong drink." Such a determination will never loose him from the binding fetters.

The one who is bound by an evil habit or has yielded to the fascinations of an alluring spirit must make a positive, definite decision, in every way possible turn from the temptation, and call upon God for help with a faith that will not waver; then deliverance is sure to come, and grace to be an overcomer.

TRIALS MADE STEPPING-STONES TO GREATER VICTORIES

The beautiful roses are protected by thorns, many of which are hidden away beneath the presentation of beauty. Roses are not often plucked without the one who would enjoy their fragrance realizing a pain by being pricked in an attempt to secure the sweet-scented flower as his own. Just why the thorns are there we do not know. Many a young recruit looks with admiration upon the veteran skill of the soldier who has been through fierce battles and has come forth as a hero. But his fame was not obtained without hardships and wounds, as the scars which he carries give testimony. About us on every side are veterans of the cross of Christ, those whose lives we admire, whose experiences we covet, but back of them no doubt are the pricking thorns in the form of trials, which have proved to be stepping-stones to the beautiful life of faith and devotion and which have graced their spiritual pathway. The roses are none the less fragrant and beautiful because of the hidden thorns beneath them. Neither is the life of a Christian less brilliant and radiant because of the trials and temptations along the way.

The enjoyment of a Christian life is what we make it. The darkest, saddest life ever known, the most dejected person in existence, the one who is surrounded constantly by infamy, blasphemy, and dark forebodings, or that one whose life has been a failure and who through adversity is doomed to spend his days behind prison-walls, can find a haven of rest in this life and in the life to come. It is through the grace of God that such can be accomplished.

No matter what your sin is or has been, you can have deliverance and peace that the world can not understand. A firm decision and trust in God will take you through by his grace. When trials come, tell the Lord about them, "casting all your cares upon him, for he careth for you." Oh the riches of his grace, the power of his love! There is an abundance in the great storehouse of our heavenly Father subject to our petitions, and he offers his heavenly riches freely and his blessings to be poured out without measure.

"Now unto him that is able to do exceeding abundantly above all that we ask or think, according to the power that worketh in us, unto him be glory in the church by Christ Jesus throughout all ages, world without end" (Eph. 3:20, 21). "Let us therefore come boldly unto the throne of grace, that we may obtain mercy, and find grace to help in time of need" (Heb. 4:16).

Zion's Bank

The following quaint verses are supposed to have been
written by Roland Hill at a time when public credit in Great
Britain was shaken by the failure of several banks.

I have a never-failing bank,

A more than golden store;

No earthly bank is half so rich;

How, then, can I be poor?

'Tis when my stock is spent and gone

And I without a groat,

I'm glad to hasten to my bank

And beg a little note.

Sometimes my Banker, smiling, says:

"Why don't you oftener come?

And when you draw a little note,

Why not a larger sum?

"Why live so niggardly and poor?

Your bank contains a plenty.

Why come and take a one-pound note,

When you might have a twenty?

"Yea, twenty thousand ten times told

Is but a trifling sum

To what your Father has laid up

Secure in Christ, his Son."

Since, then, my Banker is so rich,

I have no cause to borrow;

I'll live upon my cash today,

And draw again tomorrow.

I've been a thousand times before,

And never was rejected;

Sometimes my Banker gives me more

Than asked for or expected.

Sometimes I've felt a little proud

I've managed things so clever;

But ah! before the day is gone

I've felt as poor as ever.

Should all the banks in Britain break,

And that of England smash,

Bring in your notes to Zion's bank;

You'll surely have your cash.

And if you have but one small note,

Fear not to bring it in;

Come boldly to the bank of Grace;

The Banker is within.

All forged notes will be refused;

Man-merits are rejected;

There not a single note will pass

That God has not accepted.

This bank is full of precious notes,

All signed and sealed and free,

Though many a doubting soul may say,

"There is not one for me."

The leper had a little note—

"Lord, if you will you can";

The Banker cashed this little note,

And healed the sickly man.

We read of one young man, indeed,

Whose riches did abound;

But in this Banker's book of grace

This man was never found.

But see the wretched dying thief

Hang by the Banker's side;

He cried, "Dear Lord, remember me";

He got his cash and died.

Made in the USA
San Bernardino, CA
04 May 2016